CRAFTY CROOKS AND CONMEN

TRUE CRIME FROM WHARNCLIFFE
Foul Deeds and Suspicious Deaths Series

Barking, Dagenham & Chadwell Heath
Barnsley
Bath
Bedford
Birmingham
Black Country
Blackburn and Hyndburn
Bolton
Bradford
Brighton
Bristol
Cambridge
Carlisle
Chesterfield
Colchester
Coventry
Croydon
Derby
Dublin
Durham
Ealing
Folkestone and Dover
Grimsby
Guernsey
Guildford
Halifax
Hampstead, Holborn and St Pancras
Huddersfield
Hull

Leeds
Leicester
Lewisham and Deptford
Liverpool
London's East End
London's West End
Manchester
Mansfield
More Foul Deeds Birmingham
More Foul Deeds Chesterfield
More Foul Deeds Wakefield
Newcastle
Newport
Norfolk
Northampton
Nottingham
Oxfordshire
Pontefract and Castleford
Portsmouth
Rotherham
Scunthorpe
Southend-on-Sea
Staffordshire and The Potteries
Stratford and South Warwickshire
Tees
Warwickshire
Wigan
York

OTHER TRUE CRIME BOOKS FROM WHARNCLIFFE

A-Z of Yorkshire Murder
Black Barnsley
Brighton Crime and Vice 1800-2000
Durham Executions
Essex Murders
Executions & Hangings in Newcastle
 and Morpeth
Norfolk Mayhem and Murder

Norwich Murders
Strangeways Hanged
The A-Z of London Murders
Unsolved Murders in Victorian and
 Edwardian London
Unsolved Norfolk Murders
Unsolved Yorkshire Murders
Yorkshire's Murderous Women

Please contact us via any of the methods below for more information or a catalogue.
WHARNCLIFFE BOOKS
47 Church Street – Barnsley – South Yorkshire – S70 2AS
Tel: 01226 734555 – 734222 Fax: 01226 – 734438
E-mail: enquiries@pen-and-sword.co.uk
Website: www.wharncliffebooks.co.uk

Crafty Crooks and
CONMEN

NIGEL BLUNDELL
SUSAN BLACKHALL

First published in Great Britain in 2009 by
Wharncliffe True CRime
imprint of
Pen & Sword Books Ltd
47 Church Street
Barnsley
South Yorkshire
S70 2AS

Copyright © Nigel Blundell and Susan Blackhall 2009

ISBN 978 1 84563 077 5

The right of Nigel Blundell and Susan Blackhall to be identified as Author
of this Work has been asserted with them in accordance with the
Copyright, Designs and Patents Act 1988.

A CIP catalogue record for this book is available from the British Library.

Typeset in 11/13pt Plantin by
Mac Style, Beverley, East Yorkshire

Printed and bound in the UK by
CPI

Pen & Sword Books Ltd incorporates the imprints of Pen & Sword
Aviation, Pen & Sword Maritime, Pen & Sword Military, Wharncliffe Local
History, Pen and Sword Select, Pen and Sword Military Classics and
Leo Cooper.

For a complete list of Pen & Sword titles please contact
PEN & SWORD BOOKS LIMITED
47 Church Street, Barnsley, South Yorkshire, S70 2AS, England
E-mail: enquiries@pen-and-sword.co.uk
Website: www.pen-and-sword.co.uk

Contents

Introduction

They're crafty and cunning – every one of them a conman who would relieve you of your hard-earned cash without a qualm.

And yet what sets apart the crooks who fill the pages of this book is the manner of their crimes. It is not so much what they do but the style in which they do it that makes them memorable.

Their exploits are, of course, reprehensible. But while it would it be utterly wrong to condone their criminal artifice, it is near-impossible to not to admire their ingenuity.

If only the crooks and conmen whose crimes are catalogued here had turned their energy and expertise to honest enterprise, most of them would have been rich and famous. In the event, most ended up outcast and infamous.

Like the phoney and philanderer John Stonehouse, a politician with a glittering career ahead of him who threw it all away for greed and the love of a beautiful woman.

Or Clifford Irving, the author who fooled publishers with the 'biography' of a man he'd never met. And Frank Abagnale, the fake pilot who conned his way into airline cockpits – and into the beds of countless ladies along the way.

Joyti De-Laurey was Britain's most 'successful' female fraudster, stealing £4million from her rich employers – with the excuse: 'I've got an illness only diamonds can cure.'

More dangerous was dodgy doctor John Romulus Brinkley, who made his mark in medicine by transplanting goats' testicles onto men with the false promise that the weird operation would boost their sexual powers.

Another master of the trickster's trade was Victor Lustig, known as the 'Bouncing Czech', who was arguably the greatest conmen of the past century. Having sold the Eiffel Tower (twice) and gone on the run with the proceeds, he should have retired rich. Instead he carried on duping people and died in jail.

Conmen like Lustig have always relied on that human frailty, greed. It's said that a fool and his money are easily parted but a greedy fool is an even better bet for the confidence trickster. Other powerful lures laid by those on the wrong side of the law are lust, laziness or ambition.

The victims are as disparate a bunch of characters as the crooks and conmen who targeted them. But the confidence tricksters have one thing in common... their exploits are remembered long after their more virtuous victims are forgotten!

Chapter 1

The 'Spy' who Duped them

It is hard to believe that anyone could allow a chance encounter with a total stranger to turn their lives into a humiliating charade of fear, exploitation and degradation. But that is exactly what happened to the victims of Robert Hendy-Freegard. The former barman met people seeking excitement in their otherwise very ordinary existences then drove them to the brink of madness.

While he was power-mad, they became powerless. As he took charge of their every waking moment, they became more and more subservient. It was make-believe in the hands of a maniac. For ten years, Robert Hendy-Freegard carried out one of the most elaborate and audacious frauds in British history; his motto: 'Lies have to be big to be convincing.'

Like everything else about him, Robert Hendy-Freegard's name was a creation. Born Robert Freegard on March 1, 1977, he added the 'Hendy' later in life – a particularly cruel testament to one of his female victims. His humble birthplace, a small village near Whitwell, in Derbyshire, could not contain Hendy-Freegard for long. He was, he felt, cut out for a more rewarding life. And alongside the rather mundane occupations of working behind bars and selling cars, that is what Hendy-Freegard found when he added 'conman' and 'impostor' to his CV.

He excelled at both, first terrorising a group of students with claims that they were being hunted by the IRA, then seducing a series of women across Britain, all the while revelling in how easily people believed his claim to be a spy. Once a friendship was established, Hendy-Freegard would reveal his 'role' as an undercover agent for MI5, Special Branch or Scotland Yard, win his victims over, ask for money and then, quite literally, rule their lives. He even managed to get them to sever family links, abandon friends and undergo cruel loyalty tests. Evil

Hendy-Freegard's mind games caused mental and physical suffering almost beyond belief.

Even before he became a professional conman, Hendy-Freegard used those who trusted him. A girlfriend, teacher Alison Hopkins, lent him £1,500 after he told her a string of stories – lying also about the qualifications he had acquired at school. It was only after the couple split up that Alison realised Hendy-Freegard had been stealing money from her account, using her cash card and memorising her PIN number.

Things took a more sinister turn when Alison was stalked by her former lover and she took the desperate step of moving to Shropshire to escape him. In 1993, Hendy-Freegard was convicted at Nottingham Crown Court of three counts of theft from Alison, with a conspiracy to kidnap charge left on file – relating to an incident in which he allegedly tried to have her snatched by two accomplices. He was given a conditional discharge.

None of this was known, of course, as Hendy-Freegard continued in his job at The Swan, the pub in Newport, Shropshire, where he had gone to pursue his fleeing former girlfriend. Hendy-Freegard charmed his customers – especially the female ones. Learning that IRA gun-runner Kevin O'Donnell had studied at a local agricultural college two years' earlier and had been killed in an SAS ambush in 1992, the callous conman hit upon the basis of his brainwashing schemes. He played on the college students' fears, telling them he was a spy. Fellow bar workers laughed at him behind his back but the impressionable young people were taken in.

Three of these students, Maria Hendy, Sarah Smith and her boyfriend John Atkinson, were amongst the pub's regular customers and Hendy-Freegard quickly fell into conversation with them. He told them he was a secret agent. Over the next few years, they endured poverty, carried out bizarre missions and lived in terror. They were told not to see their family or friends because this would put them in danger; they also could not use the lavatory before him.

Both young women were seduced by Hendy-Freegard. Maria had two children with him. Was it this cruel sense of humour that had him adding her surname to his own? What is known for sure is that Maria and Sarah were persuaded to join Hendy-Freegard on a tour of Britain along with Mr Atkinson, whom they believed was suffering from a terminal illness. Once he had them on their own, Hendy-Freegard told them there was now no going back, for they were involved in an undercover operation designed to save their lives. Contracts had been taken out because of their association with him. They had to stay on the run to avoid detection.

By now, brainwashed and confused, the three allowed themselves to be moved into a 'safe house' in Peterborough. Sarah was ordered to ring home and tell her parents she wasn't going back to college because she had been offered a job with the Commercial Union insurance company.

More temporary accommodation throughout the country followed, with Hendy-Freegard feeding the three false information about each other and their families. The conman also managed to get all three to part with their cash. By the time Hendy-Freegard's crimes were discovered, he had defrauded Sarah Smith and her family of £300,000 and Mr Atkinson and his family of £390,000.

While his victims led gruelling, isolated lives under Hendy-Freegard's control, he led a much more pleasant one, holidaying in five-star luxury and buying expensive meals and designer suits with their cash.

Sarah Smith, who remained in the cruel conman's clutches for ten years, was once so hungry that she ate left-over chip batter in the fish and chip shop he had ordered her to work in. 'My world was turned upside down,' she later said. 'When I challenged Bob on why I had to work there, he told me his bosses thought I needed bringing down to earth. I had been told my boyfriend was dying, that I couldn't see my friends and family and now I had to work in a chip shop. I coped by switching off.'

When employed in a hotel, Miss Smith was only allowed to keep her tips. She would also be forced to wait at service stations and airports for up to a fortnight at a time, with as little as £10 to live on. She endured being driven around with a bucket on her head to keep her destination a secret, and noting down endless car number plates to make sure the IRA were 'not on to her'. She was ordered to pawn jewellery which had belonged to her grandmother and to empty her bank accounts to avoid being traced.

Miss Smith said: 'He told me so many lies using a mixture of charm and menace that I never knew which way was up. He knows what makes you tick and how to make you do what he wants. That's why he's so dangerous.'

On a rare meeting with their daughter, Jill and Peter Smith noted how subdued she was. 'She was tearful and difficult to talk to. She looked as if she had been mentally whipped into place,' said Mr Smith. 'She was in a bad state and sobbing. Time and time again, we begged her to come home but there was a hold and we couldn't break it.'

Wealthy farmer's son John Atkinson could only agree. He spent three years on the run, fleeing from imaginary Republican gangs. 'Hendy-Freegard ruined my life and many other people's too. He put me through hell. It was degrading and humiliating. He's very good at what he does but his motives were so pathetic and contrived you could never make it up.'

Hendy-Freegard led Atkinson to believe he was being recruited to fight the IRA. He was put into 'training' and forced to perform spurious jobs. Sometimes he would have to wait for days in a certain place for a non-existent assignation. At one point, the terrified man allowed himself to be beaten black and blue to 'toughen him up'. He was then ordered to pretend he was dying from cancer and to flee his college course. Another time, he was ordered to get a job as a barman at the same Swan pub as his tormentor and to turn up for work with his hair dyed orange and wearing a dress. Like his fellow victims, Mr Atkinson had to hand his wages straight over to Hendy-Freegard.

The poor man's family were on the brink of selling their farm in Cumbria to raise even more money when Mr Atkinson returned home in April 1997 close to a breakdown. He had decided he would rather risk being assassinated by the IRA than carrying on life as it was. He finally moved to Prague to start a new life as a teacher.

When Maria Hendy eventually found out about her lying lover's affairs and confronted him, he beat her, threatened to kill her and told her she could not talk to anyone for 'security reasons'. Miss Hendy knew just what her lover was capable of; he once smashed her teeth and then forced her to tell a dentist she had fallen downstairs.

Telling her story later, Miss Hendy said her lying, vicious lover regularly beat her. 'I put up with split lips, black eyes, broken ankles and bruised ribs,' she said. 'He spent long periods away but forbade me to have a life of my own. I became depressed and gorged on chocolate. Then he said I was fat and useless and no one would love me.'

Hendy-Freegard hid Christmas cards sent from Miss Hendy's family and kept her short of money to feed her children.

Her ordeal ended in 2001 when Hendy-Freegard admitted to an affair with another of his victims, lawyer Caroline Cowper. That was the last straw for the long-suffering mother of his children. She managed to arrange for her father to collect her and returned to the safety and sanity of her family's home in Bath. But not before one final, savage attack.

'I will never forget that night. We were at his mother's house when he came home and announced he was going to take my children and go to her [his new lover Caroline Cowper],' Miss Hendy recalled. 'I knew I had to stand up to him. I was still recovering from the beating just a month before when he punched my teeth out. He just went mad again. He came at me and his hands closed around my throat. He was strangling me.'

All the while, there were other victims suffering just like Miss Hendy. For Hendy-Freegard ran a very clever balancing act, dipping in and out of people's lives. And whenever he could, he took not only their cash but their freedom and peace of mind.

Caroline Cowper had become immediately attracted to Hendy-Freegard when he sold her a car from a showroom in Chiswick, West London, in 2000. In a customer questionnaire, she cheekily said the salesman introduced himself 'in bed' and gave him '11 out of 10 for satisfaction'.

Hendy-Freegard could not believe his luck at finding such easy prey. He went in for the kill, hanging around Miss Cowper's home and pestering her for a drink. He won sympathy by spinning a story about being brought up in poverty and how his father had died. His father was, in fact, still alive.

'I felt sorry for him,' Miss Cowper said later. 'I wasn't looking for love but I suppose I was definitely bored, and boredom is a dangerous thing. I have thought a lot about how I got lured in by Robert. The one thing with him is you could never say you were bored. He did your head in but he took me all over the place. With him, it was an adventure, but he did do these disappearing acts where he would vanish with his mobile phone switched off, which used to really irritated me.'

During their early days together, Hendy-Freegard helped Miss Cowper to trade in her £6,000 Mercedes for a £20,000 Volkswagen Golf, pocketed the difference, asked for more, persuaded her to fund a leasing business they would run together and stole £14,000 from her building society account. Once, when challenged, Hendy-Freegard said he would pay back the money once he had been paid by his MI5 bosses. Although Miss Cowper's family tried to intervene, Hendy-Freegard gave Miss Cowper a £7,000 engagement ring and took her on holiday to Brazil and Madeira. She then discovered he had been paying for these love tokens by raiding her bank account. In all, Hendy-Freegard stole £50,000.

'A lot of my friends told me there was something very weird about this chap – the fact that he was telling me he had some mysterious past,' confessed Miss Cowper. 'It did eventually begin to drive me bananas.'

Simon Young worked in a jewellery shop in Sheffield and was behind the counter when the conman called in one day. A friendship soon developed and after socialising together on a number of occasions, Hendy-Freegard 'came clean' about his espionage work. He persuaded the watchmaker to provide temporary accommodation for Sarah Smith, implying she needed a safe house.

Mr Young recalled: 'He tried to enrol me into an organisation as well as certain training. Yes, I was interested in doing government work like this, of course I was. It was every schoolboy's fantasy. Later he sent me on the training. It involved numerous different tasks.'

These included going to Manchester to buy a £1.25 can opener from a particular shop. Mr Young was given detailed instructions about which buses and trains to catch, the doors and escalators to be used and warned he would be under constant surveillance. Then he was ordered to buy a copy of *Gay Times* and openly read it on the train to London. Sheffield coach station had sold out of the magazine but Mr Young headed to the capital anyway. In his possession was the can opener. Following his orders to the letter, Mr Young went to a West End pub and asked the barman for a particular person. When told there was no one of that name there, Mr Young handed the man behind the bar the can opener and said: 'Well, when you see him, give him this.'

It was only noting Hendy-Freegard's mirth at all this that Mr Young realised he had been conned. This was confirmed when Mr Young demanded a meeting with MI5 bosses and only Hendy-Freegard turned up.

Renata Kister, a Polish company director, was seven months' pregnant and had just separated from her partner when she walked into Hendy-Freegard's London car showroom. After becoming friendly, the fraudster told Miss Kister that his MI5 bosses had ordered him to watch someone within the car dealership. He persuaded Miss Kister to buy a better car, kept the £10,000 he made on her old one and encouraged her to take out a £15,000 loan for him. Whenever she asked him for the money, he said he was awaiting payment from his secret agent bosses.

Hendy-Freegard again asked for temporary accommodation for Susan Smith, saying she was on a witness protection scheme, having fled her violent husband. He told Miss Kister that Miss Smith was Spanish and spoke no English. In turn, he told Miss Smith, whom he had convinced was being hunted by the ITA, to pretend, for security reasons, that she could not understand anything said to her.

Incredibly, the two women did not exchange a word in three months. And when Miss Kister was originally questioned by police, she refused to co-operate, believing them to be staging an MI5 loyalty test.

Leslie Gardner gave Hendy-Freegard £16,000 over a period of six years, after meeting him in a Newcastle nightclub when she was 28. She even sold her car because he needed cash to 'buy off some killers' whom he said were IRA bombers released under the Good Friday agreement. Civil servant Miss Gardner was also conned into believing Hendy-Freegard needed money to pay off IRA blackmailers: buy himself out of the police: start a new life as a taxi driver and to help his seriously-ill mother.

Three months after Hendy-Freegard gave Miss Gardner a Volkswagen Golf, she found out she owed the finance company three £260 monthly payments. Hendy-Freegard had pocketed his salesman's commission, too.

Elizabeth Bartholemew was a 22-year-old personal assistant and sales administrator at a Vauxhall car dealership in Sheffield when she met the man who would ruin her; he even managed to wreck her six-month-old marriage. Mrs Bartholemew became a regular customer of Hendy-Freegard, looking after his two daughters by Miss Hendy, while he test-drove a string of top-of-the-range cars. He gave Mrs Bartholemew expensive perfume but more importantly the attention and affection she said she did not get at home. He was, she was later to admit, 'very good in bed'.

Out of bed, Hendy-Freegard reserved some of his cruellest treatment for this victim. He took naked photographs of her, threatening to show them to her husband if she disobeyed him. Already suffering from her lover's savage temper, Mrs Bartholemew agreed not to speak to or see friends and family because of his 'threats from the IRA'. She even agreed to change her name to 'Miss Richardson', telling the deed poll officer it was because she had been molested as a child.

As 'Miss Richardson', she had to endure loyalty tests, supposedly to convince MI5 she was suitable wife material for

Hendy-Freegard. These included becoming a blonde, going without make-up and sanitary protection, sleeping in Heathrow Airport several nights at a time and living on park benches for weeks during winter. 'Sometimes I could not sleep, so I would just walk around to keep out of danger,' she recalled sadly in court.

Hendy-Freegard confiscated Miss Richardson's jacket, leaving her shivering in just a T-shirt and jeans, and made her survive on a loaf or Mars bar. Weak, thin, covered in eczema and her feet a mass of bleeding, pus-oozing sores, Miss Richardson must have cut a tragic figure in the libraries in which she sought sanctuary from the cold. She foraged in public lavatories for fresh water.

Hendy-Freegard gave the poor woman no respite; she also had to pretend to be a Jehovah's Witness, walking through London in a full Indian wedding sari complete with bangles and a painted bindi on her forehead. She was told MI5 had given her a choice of three towns in which to live, and she had to tour them, visiting shops, pubs, doctors' surgeries and hospitals before writing an extensive report.

After Hendy-Freegard told her a sniper was targeting her home, Miss Richardson crawled from room to room and spent each evening in the dark. On his orders, she took out loans for him totalling £14,500. Holding the cash in her hand, Miss Richardson could only watch as her tormentor snatched it from her, saying his MI5 bosses wanted to see him urgently. One request Miss Richardson did refuse was to change her name to that of actress Elizabeth Hurley.

Although initially refusing to co-operate with the police, it was a broken woman who stood in court to tell her traumatic tale. 'I never talked to anyone about my plight,' she said. 'I was told people would be watching my every movement. I was just waiting for him to say his bosses had given the word for us to live together. But he kept saying I had failed the tests, and until I passed we couldn't even have a sexual relationship again.'

As well as the financial loss, the ordeal cost Miss Richardson her health, marriage and self-respect.

Dr Kimberley Adams was 31 when she met Hendy-Freegard in August 2002. She made the mistake of telling him her stepmother had won the state lottery back home in America. An author and child psychologist, Miss Adams should have perhaps been able to identity the signs of someone who wasn't quite who he claimed to be. But she believed his tales, including how he was working undercover to infiltrate a dangerous criminal network: how he had to be violent on the job and how had murdered a man who threatened to expose him.

Hendy-Freegard proposed to Dr Adams after knowing her for just over a year. The proposal was not without its demands. Dr Adams was told she, too, would have to become a spy, resign from her job in Reading, Berkshire and have no contact with her family.

The cold and calculating conman stepped up his treatment of Dr Adams. He told her they would live in a Scottish lighthouse for twenty-five years, monitoring Russian submarines in the North Sea. But first she had to undergo various tests and change her identity. All the while, MI5 and Scotland Yard would examine and evaluate everything she had ever done and she must tell him about all her sexual encounters – in detail.

When Dr Adams confessed to kissing a man shortly after meeting Hendy-Freegard, he flew into a rage, saying she was such a bad woman that it was better her son was dead than have a mother like her. 'He said if I refused to kill my son, he would have to bury him alive,' a tearful Dr Adams was later to tell a crowded courtroom.

Then Hendy-Freegard said he had taken out a contract on both Dr Adams and her son, who was at school back in America. He told her she had sacrificed her son's life with her lies and that at the end of the night 'I would be glad to be dead'. Dr Adams was left shaking. Yet she still surrendered to Hendy-Freegard's treatment. He flushed her anti-depressant tablets down a toilet and sent her to live with her 'very humble' mother for three months in Worksop, Nottinghamshire. At one point in their bizarre relationship, Dr Adams spent three weeks hiding in a bathroom, locked in by her lover.

When Dr Adams said she did not want to spend 25 years in a lighthouse, Hendy-Freegard insisted the arrangements had already been made and that she would have to repay the state £80,000. This set off a chain of events. Dr Adams telephoned her father John, a film producer in Omaha, Nebraska, and asked for £20,000 for 'spy school'. He in turn, approached his ex-wife Anne Hodgins, Dr Adams's stepmother and £11m lottery winner, for the cash. But then Dr Adams was ordered to ask for money yet again. This time it was for £10,000 for Hendy-Freegard to re-sit his spy exams.

Such was the hold the fraudster was able to exert on everyone, that Dr Adams and her parents – just like other victims – at first refused to help police believing them to be double agents. The man whose vicious con was described in court as 'an odyssey of deceit' bought himself seven BMWs as well as an £80,000 Aston Martin Volante and Rolex watches. He also bought suits, holidays and fine meals with his victims' money. Somehow, he managed to get them all to turn to their families for cash. His mixture of menace and charm had them in 'safe houses' around the country while he lived his James Bond world of fantasy.

It was no wonder Hendy-Freegard earned himself the nickname 'The Puppetmaster'. His treatment of his female victims ran to a pattern. At first the perfect boyfriend, handsome, attentive and generous, he would then disappear for weeks and start to drop hints that he was not just a car salesman but something far more exciting. None of his women victims knew about his relationships with the others. He would often use one woman's money to woo another with gifts and expensive dinners. He promised marriage but it never happened. He did not balk at stopping on motorways and threatening to throw his female companion out of the car. At the end of his ten-year terror reign Hendy-Freegard had stolen between half a million and one million pounds from his victims.

It was a 'sting' as devious as the conman's own way of working that brought his reign to an end. Caroline Cowper had already sued Hendy-Freegard and reported him to police. Then Maria Hendy and John Atkinson came forward.

What the Crown Prosecution Service described as an 'ambitious arrest strategy' was in place by April 2003. Dr Kimberley Adams' mother was to fly in to London from America with a large amount of money for Hendy-Freegard. This was to be offered in exchange for the opportunity to see her daughter. The plan worked perfectly and on May 23, 2002, Hendy-Freegard was arrested at Heathrow.

Dr Adams was in a car close by. Although at first uncooperative with the police, she finally told them her lover had left a briefcase in a hotel room in France. The briefcase was found to contain documents belonging to Sarah Smith, Renata Kister, Elizabeth Richardson and Lesley Gardner. Eventually all victims were traced.

On June 23, 2005, after an eight-month trial, Robert Hendy-Freegard was convicted on 20 counts: one of kidnapping Sarah Smith and one of kidnapping John Atkinson; ten charges of theft, five of obtaining money by deception and three of procuring the execution of a valuable security by deception.

Some of 'the Puppetmaster's' victims were in court to see him sentenced to life on September 6. Sarah Smith, then 36, could not hide her relief. But she said she feared some unknown victims could still be living in poverty. 'He tried to ship me abroad, and if he managed to do that with anyone else, they could still be there, without money or passports, unaware of this case,' she said. 'There could be a number of people who have not come forward.'

Caroline Cowper, 38, was also relieved at the verdict. 'Life is an excellent sentence,' she said. 'But it's a shame it couldn't be longer. He is a danger to society and there are lots of vulnerable people out there. The streets will be safer while he's locked away.'

Meanwhile, Hendy-Freegard, who had shown no pity for his victims, lounged in one of the dock chairs as Judge Deva Pillay told him: 'In my judgement, the several verdicts of the jury in this case represented a vindication of your victims and a telling testament to their courage, tenacity and spirit to overcome adversity, despite the depths of despair to which they were driven by you. It was plain to me as I listened to the evidence for many months that you are an egotistical and opinionated confidence trickster who has shown not a shred of remorse or compassion for the degradation and suffering to which your victims were subjected.'

A life sentence was no more than Hendy-Freegard deserved, said the judge, because of the heinous nature of his crimes against those who had 'fallen prey to his devious charm'. He added: 'There are substantial grounds for believing you will remain a serious danger to the public and to women in particular.'

There was a further twist to this unsavoury tale, however. At the Court of Appeal in April 2007, Robert Hendy-Freegard was cleared on a legal technicality of the two counts of kidnap. The Lord Chief Justice ruled that the kidnapping convictions were unsafe because the victims, Sarah Smith and John Atkinson, were not physically deprived of their liberty. It was not enough for the victims to be psychologically trapped, he said. It was believed that the two were suffering from Stockholm Syndrome, by which kidnap victims fall in love with their captor.

The dropping of the two kidnap charges meant Hendy-Freegard could no longer be a 'lifer' but instead serve the remaining nine-year jail term for fraud and theft. But taking into account the time he had already been in prison, Hendy-Freegard would soon be at large again, free to start ensnaring innocent people.

It was yet another bitter blow for those who had suffered so much at his hands. Said Sarah Smith: 'What happened to me could have happened to anybody. And that is proved by the fact that so many people were taken in by him. Whichever way you look at it, I was deprived of my liberty for ten years. Whether it be physically or mentally, I was still prevented from having my own liberty and everything that it means to live a normal life.'

The police, who had worked so hard to bring 'The Puppetmaster' to justice, were equally dismayed. Said Metropolitan Police investigating officer, Detective Sergeant Mark Simpson: 'These ten people were under someone's control totally. How can someone lose ten years of their life at someone else's behest? How can they do that if they weren't falsely imprisoned? The victims are going to be very worried that he is going to come and find them and their family. Many of them are still psychologically damaged.'

Miss Hendy was more forgiving. Although admitting it was a relief not to be forever looking over her shoulder, she added: 'I feel pity for him because he never really knew how to love.'

CHAPTER 2

The Star-struck Conman

The headline summed it up: 'He Conned the Society Crowd but Died Alone'. For that was indeed the sad ending for a man who fell into the life of a celebrity imposter and fraud on a whim, then milked his fabricated existence for all it was worth.

Little is known about the early life of American con-artist David Hampton. He was born in Buffalo, New York State, in 1964, the son of an attorney. But the city did not suit Hampton in his desire to find fame and fortune, and he left at the first opportunity because 'no one who lived there was glamorous or fabulous or outrageously talented'.

Hampton moved to New York City in 1981 to pursue his ambition of being an actor and dancer. He certainly fulfilled the former – although not in a professional or legitimate way. For it was just two years later that homosexual Hampton stumbled upon his most infamous ruse. When he and a friend were refused entry to New York's legendary Studio 54 club, the two men came up with an idea. Hampton's friend would pretend to be actor Gregory Peck's son and Hampton would pose as the son of noted black actor Sidney Poitier. They went to the nearby Plaza Hotel, borrowed a limousine and returned to the club under their new identities. They were ushered in immediately.

Once he had tasted the privileges that being 'David Poitier' offered, Hampton knew he just had to maintain the lie. He managed to get free meals in restaurants by telling the manager that he was there to meet his father. After finishing his meal, he would say that his father must have been detained on business, and the restaurant would promptly pick up the bill.

After managing to get hold of an address book from a passing friend who lived on New York's elite Upper East Side, Hampton also persuaded at least a dozen well-known people to let him stay with them. These included actress Melanie Griffith, actor Gary Sinise, designer Calvin Klein and John Jay Iselin, president of America's WNET public broadcasting station. All the while, Hampton maintained the fiction that he was a friend of his host's children: that he had just missed his plane to Los Angeles and his luggage was on it, or that his belongings had been stolen.

Hampton accepted money and clothes, regaled his hosts with stories about his famous father and even offered them bit parts in films he said were directed by Poitier. One duped victim was Osborn Elliot, the dean of the Columbia University Graduate School of Journalism and a former editor of *Newsweek*. Elliot and his wife Inger evicted Hampton when they found him in bed with a man he'd smuggled into their apartment the very first morning he stayed there.

Several times, Hampton tried to inveigle himself into the office of Andy Warhol but the artist saw through his patter every time. Hampton was later to remark: 'Andy was a con-artist himself. One salesman can always spot another.'

Hampton was arrested and convicted of his frauds and ordered to pay restitution of $4,500 to his various victims. He was also banned from New York City. After refusing to comply with these terms, he was sentenced to 21 months in prison.

It was a colourful lifestyle crying out to be immortalized. And that is exactly what happened. When Osborn Elliot told his dramatist friend John Guare how he and his wife had been conned, Guare saw it as the basis for a play. He was further intrigued after reading newspaper reports about Hampton's exploits and another arrest (his seventh) in October 1983. The result was *Six Degrees of Separation* which opened on Broadway in 1990. It was hailed by notoriously tough *New York Times* critic Frank Rich as 'a masterpiece that captures New York as Tom Wolfe did in *Bonfire of the Vanities*'. The play was nominated for four Tony Awards.

The play also presented another golden opportunity for confidence trickster Hampton. He was on holiday in Hawaii when he heard about it and rushed back to ensure he was at the centre of publicity. Hampton held court, gave press interviews and gatecrashed the play's opening-night party. 'I know how to waltz into a room, darling,' he told fellow guests.

But none of this was enough for the fame-seeking, money-grabbing Hampton. Incredibly, he had the gall to hire celebrity lawyer Richard Golub and file a $100 million lawsuit against Guare, claiming that because the play made use of incidents in his life, he was entitled to compensation and damages. Also cited in Hampton's civil suit were the Lincoln Centre Theatre where the play was performed, the Lincoln Centre for the Performing Arts, the play's producer Bernard Gersten, Random House which published the text of the play and MGM-Pathe Communications which bought the film rights.

He was, Hampton told the State Supreme Court of Manhattan at the 1991 hearing, entitled to 'the fruits of his labour'. But judge Justice Edward. H Lehner gave Hampton short shrift with the retort: 'Society's response to one whose labours are in violation of its penal laws is punishment, not reward.' The judge found that, although some of Hampton's traits could be found in the play's main character, Mr Guare had not unlawfully exploited him. The court also rejected Hampton's reasoning that his personality should be afforded the same protection as copyrights, trademarks or patents.

None of this pleased Hampton and he went on to appeal against the ruling. He lost again. Five judges at the New York State Appellate Division upheld the earlier ruling that Hampton was not entitled to civic damages for the fictional use of his story. They agreed that: 'Works of fiction and satire do not fall within the narrow scope of the statutory phrases "advertising" and "trade".'

Hampton may have left court displeased, but the verdict became a landmark one. Laura Handman, a lawyer with Lankenau Kovner & Kurtz which defended John Guare, Random House and MGM-Pathe commented: 'The decision is an important victory for all authors of literature who draw to varying degrees upon real life. It also is a reaffirmation that plays and movies are not merely commercial products but works of expression protected by the First Amendment.'

Hampton's lawyer Richard Golub still maintained that *Six Degrees of Separation* was not constitutionally protected fiction but 'non-fiction, a transparent *roman a clef* – it's a work of fact'. He added that although he was not attempting to inhibit writers' freedom of speech, 'if they write about you in this way, they should have to pay for it'.

A bitter Hampton later hounded John Guare with death threats and attempts to exhort money from him – and found himself in court once again. The focus of the trial at Manhattan Criminal Court was a series of phone calls that Hampton made to John Guare's home. The recorded calls were played in court. In one of them, Hampton was heard to say: 'I would strongly advise you to give me some money or you start counting your days. I suggest you count out some cash and allot it to me legally and rightfully, like you should do like a gentleman, or I am going to do something so that you won't be able to walk on stage and accept any awards.'

Assistant District Attorney Valerie Avrin agreed that the message constituted a threat. 'There isn't any doubt about it,' she said. Defending Hampton, Ronald Kuby said he did not deny that his client placed the calls, but disagreed with the prosecution's claim they were threatening. He said: 'In the give-and-take and hurly-burly of city life, often speech is rough and sometimes annoying. But it is not criminal. We hear them once and we will hear them again.'

Incredibly, the jury took Hampton's side. It acquitted him of the charge of harassing John Guare in an effort to obtain money from him and 'dead-locked' – failed to reach a majority verdict – on a second charge of straight harassment. It was the right verdict, agreed Mr Kuby because his client's only intent 'was to get some recompense for what Guare had taken from him'.

Hampton's conman career continued, in between attempts to make it as an actor – and despite him swearing his fraudulent days were over. In 1991, in a bid to get work, he told the business manager of a theatre that he was the actor who had played the role of the bogus Sidney Poitier's son in *Six Degrees of Separation*. The suspicious manager called the police but when Hampton was later caught he simply shrugged, denied knowing the man and said he must have been the victim of someone impersonating the legendary

David Hampton. 'You know, I had this trouble before,' he told the police.

Hampton travelled around America until the late 1990s using a range of aliases including Patrick Owens, Antonio Jones or just plain David. He came across a lot of men who, even if they had heard of his notoriety, had never seen a photograph of him in the press. This enabled Hampton to carry on conning.

In spring 1996, Hampton arrived in Seattle, Washington, posing as Antonio de Montilio, the son of a wealthy District of Columbia physician – and because of Hampton's skin colouring, it was easy to believe he was the Puerto Rican he claimed to be. Always ready to embellish his tales, Hampton claimed to have been mugged on arrival in Seattle, where he was meant to be interviewing top businessman Bill Gates for *Vogue* magazine. He said his wallet had been stolen and nothing could be replaced straight away as it was the weekend. Hampton managed to convince two friends of this story, without either knowing he was 'working' the other. Another victim was a local actor called Justin Baird, specially chosen by Hampton for his usefulness as an official looking after funds from 'Bunny Brigade' charitable volunteers returning from their collection rounds.

One of Hampton's last victims – or rather one of the last known to the police – was Peter Bedevian, who went out on a date with a man he knew as David Hampton-Montilio in October 2001. Before heading to a restaurant, Hampton said he wanted to take Mr Bedevian to a 9/11 celebrity concert but did not have enough money with him. The gullible man withdrew £500 from a cash dispenser and gave it to Hampton, who went through the charade of dashing into a hotel to buy the tickets from 'friends from LA who were in town'.

The conman and his dupe then sat down to eat – and Mr Bedevian learned at first-hand about Hampton's persuasive *modus operandi*. 'He was a charming companion, able to pick out a little information, and extrapolate and use it to make me feel even more comfortable,' he told friends. After dinner, Hampton ordered two $24 shots of fine Scotch before excusing himself to use the bathroom – and never coming back. He left Mr Bedevian with a $400 dinner bill and the need to press charges to get his $1,000 back. The man then had the humiliating task of identifying Hampton through a two-way mirror at a police station. But incredibly, such was the conman's charm, he summed up his brush with Hampton as 'one of the best dates I ever went on'.

A film of Hampton's exploits, adapted from the original play, was made in 1993 and starred Will Smith. One co-star, Stockard Channing who had appeared in the stage version, was nominated for an Oscar for best actress for her role as a wealthy Manhattan socialite taken in by the imposter.

In between his jail sentences, Hampton regularly gave interviews for the television programme *The Justice Files*, calling his good friend Ronald Kuby for assistance. 'He would often call me for advice,' said the lawyer. 'All I could tell him was to stop doing these things!' Another friend and lawyer, Susan Tipograph, said of Hampton: 'New York was the place for him. In his mind, the fabulous people lived in New York City. I'm a 52-year-old overweight lawyer with bad knees and clubbing is not my thing. But we had a very regular friendship. We had lunch together. We had a very unfabulous friendship. Mr Hampton gave enjoyment even when he did bad.'

It was Ms Tipograph who cleaned out the small hospital room in which Hampton died, aged 39, of AIDs complications in June 2003. She said of her friend: 'David, like many of us, had a real need to be somebody important and special. He did stuff to be somebody, in his mind; somebody important, somebody fabulous. To me he was fabulous.'

Hampton had wanted to write a book about his life, he had told visitors to his bedside at New York's Beth Israel Hospital. It was not to be, but he had already enjoyed notoriety enough, and so many knew his story already. Hampton did not really gain much financially from his confidence tricks — simply tasting the high life on as many occasions as fate would allow.

Ronald Kuby summed Hampton up thus: 'David took a great joy in living the life he lived. It was performance art on the world's smallest possible stage, usually involving an audience of only one or two. When pretending to be somebody else, he dazzled people. For an evening or a couple of days, he mesmerised people by bringing them into his totally fictitious world of stardom.'

Of course, there would not have been a David Hampton story at all if anyone had bothered to check that Sidney Poitier never had a son – only daughters.

CHAPTER 3

Secretary's Secret Stash

It is one of those quotes that will go down in high-profile criminal history. 'I've got an illness only diamonds can cure.' The words were spoken by Joyti De-Laurey, the secretary with the dubious claim to being Britain's most successful – if that is the right word – female fraudster. She stole £4 million from her employers (one single transaction alone was in the sum of £2.25 million) and spent a lot of it living life to the full.

It was a feat that, although of course was nothing more than theft on a grand scale, nevertheless earned Mrs De-Laurey some respect as a very over-confident confidence trickster and high-achiever when it came to accounting. During her trial, De-Laurey was actually cheered as she travelled around London. If mega-rich companies didn't miss their millions, the public perception went, then they deserved to be robbed. 'I don't want to sound arrogant,' she later said. 'I know I committed a crime, but I received over 700 letters of support after I was convicted.'

De-Laurey was born in London in 1970, destined to be spoiled and to enjoy the high-life. She was the only child of two Indian professionals (her mother was a doctor) and was privately educated at a school in Hampstead, north London. But De-Laurey did not go on to university, desperate instead to start earning. Her early career path was quite humble and she worked in a series of administrative jobs in car showrooms before marrying chauffeur Anthony De-Laurey in 1996. De-Laurey said of their marriage: 'I think she was supposed to marry a rich Indian man but she is too headstrong to be told what to do by anyone else.' A son, Max, was born a year later. Family life should have been good, but the couple's sandwich bar business failed, prompting De-Laurey to seek more financially rewarding opportunities.

The perfect job came along in 1998 when De-Laurey walked through the imposing doors of investment bank Goldman Sachs. She was only a temporary secretary on an hourly rate of £7.50 but she was in a wondrous world where money really was no object. De-Laurey may have come from a privileged background herself but she was now astonished to realise just what fortunes could be earned – and spent. Spending half a million pounds on a birthday party was not unusual. But that was nothing compared to the £50 million worth of shares the 220 partners of Goldman Sachs each got when the investment bank floated in 1999.

What was to become De-Laurey's dream job arrived soon after when she was appointed as permanent personal assistant to one of the bank's key figures, Jennifer Moses, who was married to Goldman director Ron Beller. Estimates of De-Laurey's salary range from £38,000 a year to £50,000, the latter being her own figure. That was not a bad wage at all for a PA – but it was going to get even better. Given the responsibility of paying Ms Moses' and Mr Beller's household and personal bills meant De-Laurey had access to their cheque books. She made out cheques for them to sign, made personal shopping appointments for Ms Moses, booked beauty treatments and arranged holidays.

The couple were later to deny that secretaries and personal assistants were allowed to forge their bosses' signatures on cheques but another secretary, Sophie Pemberton, testified it was common practice in the company 'in order to get things done'. Indeed, De-Laurey said she did it regularly, particularly if a bill came in and the couple were out of the country. This led to De-Laurey taking things one step further. Just as a test exercise, she wrote herself a £4,000 cheque from Jennifer Moses's account. She later said: 'I just wanted to see if I could do it. I don't think I regarded it as a crime until it cleared. That was when I knew it was wrong. I kept it in my account for two months.'

De-Laurey then withdrew £1,000 from the Woolwich bank opposite her employers' offices and walked to a *Waterstones* bookshop where she spent £400. That £4,000 was the smallest sum De-Laurey was to steal in one go from Ms

Moses; the largest was £28,000. 'There was no skill involved in taking money from Jen and I took over £1.5 million from her,' De-Laurey was later to relate. 'I just started forging Ron and Jen's signatures on personal cheques and putting it into my account. It was unbelievable that they did not know what I was doing... It was a bit addictive... it was so easy. I got a huge buzz from knowing they had no idea what I was doing.'

De-Laurey forged 73 cheques in three months. If there was any guilt about stealing from bosses who treated her well, she did not show it. Although admitting 'sometimes they could be really warm', she also resented the fact she had to 'drop everything' if they needed her. Her husband once complained: 'Jen would be on the phone constantly, asking Jot to do this, to do that. Once, Jen even rang from a hotel room in Hong Kong to get Jot to sort out her air conditioning.'

Although De-Laurey never actually worked for Ron Beller, she was 'loaned' to him by Jennifer Moses to carry out odd jobs. De-Laurey was sent out to comb London for special ingredients for dinner parties, had to set up 'personal shopper' appointments in New York department stores, oversee builders renovating the couple's London home, organise bill-paying and field personal telephone calls.

Mr Beller had such trust in De-Laurey that he gave her the job of overseeing the arrangements for his wife's £500,000 fortieth birthday party in Rome. For this particular task, De-Laurey was paid £5,000 and received a gift of £800 worth of jewellery. Once, De-Laurey asked Ms Moses for a personal loan of £40,000 and this was given interest free. The loan was repaid using Ms Moses' own money.

Such was their trust in De-Laurey that, when Ms Moses and Mr Beller left Goldman Sachs early in 2001, they offered her a job as their personal assistant on a salary of £52,000. De-Laurey turned the offer down, choosing instead to go for 'promotion'. She then went on holiday with her husband who recalled: 'We stayed in a five-star Beverley Hills Hotel. But she told me we had got a brilliant price because Goldman Sachs did loads of business with them.'

De-Laurey always maintained that neither her husband nor family knew about her thefts. 'They just assumed I was doing so brilliantly at work that I was being greatly rewarded,' she said. This would be vehemently disputed in court. As outlined by the prosecution: 'Joyti's new wealth was what you might properly describe as conspicuous. And plainly those who knew her – her husband and mother – knew she had no legitimate means of accidentally acquiring wealth on the scale of £4 million.'

Upon her return from her American holiday, De-Laurey went to work for another Goldman Sachs director, Scott Mead, an American investment banker best known for masterminding the £100 billion takeover of German company Mannesmann by Vodafone in 2000. At one point, Mr Mead, who owned houses in Paris, Manhattan and London, was said to be worth £120 million. Thanks to his assistant's 'help yourself' approach to her job, he was soon £3 million worse off. De-Laurey used her forgery skills to write Mr Mead's signature on a string of transfer authorities, siphoning up to £2.5 million at a time from supposedly secure New York investments.

Just as with her previous bosses, De-Laurey duped Scott Mead by asking him to give signed authorisation on legitimate money transfers before attaching secondary pages with instructions for her own embezzled transfers. She would forge signatures on the extra pages. Seeing all incoming mail, De-Laurey was also able to vet money transfer information and withhold relevant pages from her employers.

Of course, there was no point stealing millions unless one lived like a millionaire. And that is exactly what De-Laurey did. She admitted buying five properties. Two were in Cyprus: a £750,000 villa which came with a New Range Rover for her husband, and the other in her mother's name. Another property, in Essex, was bought, said De-Laurey, for a friend who had hit hard times. A further two homes were bought in Cheam, Surrey. It is believed, however, that as many as eleven houses were purchased. Then there were the cars, including a Saab convertible, a Chrysler Grand Voyager and a Volkswagen Golf. De-Laurey had just put a deposit down on a £175,000 Aston Martin V12 Vanquish when she was arrested. A £150,000 power boat was ordered, but again not delivered because of the discovery of De-Laurey's fraudulent life.

Other luxuries she splashed out on included flying lessons costing £2,000, first-class travel, a trip to Memphis with another secretary to occupy £5,000 ringside seats at a major boxing match, a grand wardrobe of designer clothes and a splendid £300,000 collection of jewellery – including one £18,000 'haul' on a single trip to Cartier. The jewellery items were not 'ostentatious', said De-Laurey, allowing her to wear them in the company of those at work who had inadvertently paid for them.

She later said: 'People working with me fourteen hours a day didn't suspect a thing. The diamonds and jewellery were a short but furious splurge of going crazy. What's really nice is being able to phone Cartier and say "I want that!" and just put it on your debit card and know it's going to go through. That bit was fun.'

Perhaps as a sop to her conscience, De-Laurey made a £10,000 donation to a charity for sick children. This generous gesture was somewhat hollow considering it was someone else's money. Nor could it re-balance the lie De-Laurey had told her employers to ensure continual good treatment – that she was suffering from cancer.

Where was it all to end? As the spending spree rolled on, the glorified secretary began laying plans to leave Britain and start a new life abroad. De-Laurey had previously told Jennifer Moses that she was buying a house in Cyprus because she had been recruited to work for the Archbishop of Nicosia. There was no job, of course, but there was £2 million in a Cypriot bank account in her maiden name of Schahhou. Shortly afterwards, Anthony De-Laurey resigned from his job, telling his bosses he had to go to Cyprus 'due to a change in family circumstances'.

De-Laurey nearly got away with her easy-stealing, high-spending lifestyle. For by this time, the thefts from Jennifer Moses and Ron Beller had gone undetected for three years. But unluckily for her, after handing in her notice at Goldman Sachs, Scott Mead decided to make a substantial financial gift to his old college Harvard and went through one of his bank accounts – and discovered that the figures just did not add up. The income balances were much lower that they should have been, and in one account, there was not enough money for Mr Mead to make his gift. This led him to examine other accounts – including one he didn't even know existed.

According to De-Laurey, at first Mr Mead asked her to give some of the money back and she tried to refund half a million pounds from her Cyprus bank. But with ill-timing, it was a bank holiday on the island, so what might have been De-Laurey's golden opportunity to escape arrest did not happen. At 7.30am on May 2, 2002, she arrived for work to be confronted by Mr Mead and Jim King, head of security at Goldman Sachs. She claimed that her boss mouthed the word 'sorry' to her – but Mr Mead might dispute this. He later said: 'Every day De-Laurey would sit opposite me, sending me e-mails about how I was the best boss in the world. And every day she was ripping me off.'

De-Laurey's husband remembered the day of her arrest well. 'I hadn't heard from Jot all day but assumed she was busy as usual. Then at about 8pm, just when I was wondering where she was, two police officers turned up in a van telling me they had a warrant to search the house.'

After her departure, detectives searching De-Laurey's office discovered handwritten notes addressed to God. One read: 'Dear God, Please protect me. I need one more helping of what's mine... and then I must cut down and cease in time all the plundering.' Another read: 'Dear God, I'm so scared. I just hope and pray that all is well and that my concern is not founded... I don't want to lose Jen's trust over anything. Please protect me.'

After a brief spell in police cells and London's Holloway Prison, De-Laurey was granted bail, but only after signing an affidavit admitting to the amounts of money she had stolen, in order for Jennifer Moses, Ron Beller and Scott Mead to recover it. In the affidavit, De-Laurey wrote: 'I now realise that what I have done is completely wrong and in hindsight I am completely at a loss to understand what on earth possessed me to do as I did. I wish I had been found out before. I wish to do everything that I can to make amends.' Meanwhile, De-Laurey's husband and mother were arrested on charges of money-laundering.

But De-Laurey's earlier remorse left her by the time her high-profile trial began nineteen months later, when she appeared in court to deny four charges of using a false instrument (such as forging cheques) and sixteen counts of obtaining a money transfer by deception. The total value of her fraud was £4,303,259. At the opening of the trial at London's Southwark Crown Court in January 2004, Mr Stuart Trimmer, for the prosecution, said of De-Laurey: 'She appeared to be a very competent, very worthwhile, valuable employee. But in fact, what she was doing was dishonesty to an outstanding scale.' De-Laurey, had, said Mr Trimmer, enjoyed a way of life with 'the trappings of someone who has considerable wealth'.

De-Laurey's defence team argued that she believed Ms Moses, Mr Beller and Mr Mead were fully aware that she was taking money and that she was doing so with their consent as payment for the additional services she had provided. In the case of Mead, the defence alleged that the £3.3 million she had taken from him was 'hush money' for covering up the married father-of-five's affair with a lawyer at a City firm. Scott Mead's response was clear: 'I deny entirely, completely and totally that my personal life had anything to do whatsoever with the criminality.' He added that he found the suggestion 'absolutely repulsive'. During his evidence, Mr Mead did confess, however: 'I have a lot of things going against me. I'm wealthy, I'm American. I work in the City.'

In April 2004, after sixteen weeks of evidence, De-Laurey was convicted on twenty counts of fraud, being described as 'duplicitous, deceitful and thoroughly dishonest'. She was sentenced to seven years in prison. Despite protesting their innocence of the money-laundering charges, 50-year-old Anthony De-Laurey received an 18-month jail sentence and De-Laurey's 68-year-old mother, GP Dr Devi Schahhou, a suspended sentence.

De-Laurey was initially sent back to Holloway Prison, where she twice tried to kill herself. It was despair over not only what she had brought upon herself, but also at being separated from her son. In a magazine interview after her release in 2007, she said: 'What was cool about the whole thing – I was on bail for nineteen months – was that I started to be a real mum. Then I went to prison. I know it was my own doing but that really hurt. I took an overdose and I took it to die. I took the pills in with me.'

De-Laurey served the latter part of her sentence at Send Prison in Surrey. It was another period of total despair. She told *You* magazine: 'You get far too much time to think in prison. I had to change, but did I need three-and-half years in order to do so?' During her time in prison, De-Laurey's son lived with her mother-in-law then she and her husband separated. 'I needed to get out of my marriage. Big mistake, my marriage,' she said.

Despite all she had done, there was still a lingering public sympathy for De-Laurey, whose sentence had caused some controversy. One report noted that, compared to men convicted of similar charges, she had got a rough deal 'with a sentence far harsher than that handed out to the average fraudster'. In the UK, the average sentence for fraud-related crimes of more than £1 million is 3.3 years – less than half De-Laurey's sentence. Another scathing report stated: 'The reality is that most bankers have dull lives, working eighteen-hour days if they are lucky. For Moses, Mead and Beller, the curious incident of the missing millions gives them something they probably never had before – human interest. For that alone, they should have let De-Laurey keep the money.'

De-Laurey had her own opinion of her crime and punishment. She said: 'They [the victims] could afford to lose the money and everyone knows I could never do this again. I am being punished because I dared to take from people like them. That's not the way it's meant to be. I do believe the crime seems almost too audacious for a woman. And I made two senior male business partners of one of the world's largest merchant banks look like total pricks.'

After her release from jail, De-Laurey got a more modest £14,500-a-year job as an assistant at the London-based Koestler Trust, a charity promoting the arts to prisoners. Her home was a two-bedroom flat in Cheam – previously bought with the proceeds of her fraud. De-Laurey described the Goldman Sachs lawyers as 'pretty decent' to allow her to keep the flat. She said: 'I have use of it while my son is in full-time education. I cover the maintenance costs, which is good because I don't see why the state should have to house me.'

De-Laurey said it is now hard to believe she acted like she did – 'but I just wanted to spend,' she said. 'I'm not going to lie and say spending that amount wasn't fun, because it was, OK? I'm human. I didn't spend all of it, though. I don't think I spent even half of what I took. But I emotionally destroyed my mother and son. She had a huge sense of disappointment, also of needless self-blame. And Max sees a child psychologist. We talk about it. We have to. Max gets very angry with me. So the thing that stops me from ever doing it again isn't just my will, but that I would lose my son, my mother and my close friends.'

The business pages in newspapers described the De-Laurey case as 'perhaps the low point in the history of Goldman Sachs' – also known in the money market as 'Goldmine Sachs' and 'Golden Sachs'. Founded in New York in 1869 by Marcus Goldman, a Jewish immigrant, (his son-in-law, Samuel Sachs, joined later that century) it had only once before experienced a rocky time when, because of its high trading risks, it almost collapsed during the 1929 Wall Street Crash. Three-quarters of a century later, its easy-to-rob reputation was overshadowed by the fact it had enjoyed a record year. So much so that it would be paying bonuses of 'unprecedented magnitude' to its 4,500 London employees. One report stated: 'With £9 billion to share around the world – an increase of forty per cent from 2005, itself an exceptional year – the average employee here will receive £319,000. And that average includes everyone. Many will receive at least £1 million, and the real stars several times that.' All this added weight to what defence barrister Jeremy Dein had said – that De Laurey's trial exposed the lifestyles of individuals who were 'wealthy to the point that is the stuff of fairy tales'.

De-Laurey herself said of her time at Goldman Sachs: 'There is no culture, only vultures. The world of investment banking is such a bizarre place. No one person is worth all the money they are potentially able to earn. I look back at the person I was when I did this with a mixture of affection and irritation because of the daring of the whole thing. It was quite a feat, although at the time I felt as if I was taking it in my stride.'

Her working years with Goldman Sachs now seems like a dream. But the reality is that Joyti De-Laurey will forever be known as the secretary behind Britain's biggest female-operated fraud. She said: 'I've given back everything they wanted. I've not been difficult. I've told them things. Now I'm not financially secure but I'm emotionally secure.'

CHAPTER 4

Scourge of the Sex Surgeon

When it came to Dr John Brinkley, the saying 'there's life in the old goat yet' could not have been more apt. For goats were exactly what the quack doctor knew about – goats and their potential for making men feel life was very much worth living again. For Dr Brinkley made his mark in medicine by removing the testicles from the animals and transplanting them onto men who, delicately put, needed renewed sexual potency.

It didn't seem to matter that Brinkley was a drunk, a charlatan and quite often a killer – his patients dying of all sorts of infections through his medical malpractices. To countless males, he was their saviour.

John Romulus Brinkley was born on July 8, 1885, near Beta, Jackson County, North Carolina. He later changed his middle name to Richard. Brinkley's parents died when he was very young and he went to live with an aunt, attending a tiny, one-room school in Tuckasiegee. A bright boy, Brinkley earned himself a diploma, went on to further education and, in later years, attended the Bennett Medical College of Chicago and the Eclectic Medical University of Kansas City from which he obtained a medical licence.

By the time he started to operate on people, Brinkley was on his second marriage. He wed Sally Wike in 1908 and the couple had three children. They divorced in 1913 and he then married Minnie Telitha Jones, with whom he had a son. In 1918 Brinkley began the surgery that he claimed would restore virility and fertility by implanting the glands of goats in his male patients – at a cost of £325 per operation.

Employed in 1917 as a house doctor at the Swift meatpacking company in Kansas, Brinkley had become fascinated by the vigorous mating of goats destined for the slaughterhouse. These activities were recalled when Brinkley set up in private practice in Milford, Kansas, where a farmer named Stittsworth came to see him complaining of flagging libido. The dubious doctor was only half-joking when he told the man that what he needed was some goat glands and so was not fazed when his patient replied: 'So, Doc, put 'em in. Transplant 'em.' Brinkley was on the way to earning the name 'The Milford Messiah'.

The procedure was a relatively simple one. A patient – and they were indeed, normally Midwest farmers – would check into Brinkley's private hospital, pay the fee and then be escorted to a rear building where he could choose the goat he liked the look of. The poor, unfortunate creature was then summarily castrated, its testicles tipped into a slit cut in the man's scrotum and the incision quickly sutured. If all went well, the man did not suffer any infection and would go on to believe that the operation had had some affect on his sexual performance.

What actually happened was the patients' bodies would typically absorb the goat gonads as foreign matter; the organs were never accepted as part of the body since they were simply placed into the male testicle sac.

All the men were sent home with bottles of Brinkley's 'Prescription 1020', which was just coloured water that he sold them at a mark-up of 9,200 per cent. That is if they survived the operating table. For there were many occasions when Brinkley's patients died through inept surgery and infection – especially when Brinkley resorted to using rotting goats' testicles and his incisions turned gangrenous. Luckily for Brinkley, he was also in charge of signing their death certificates.

But as one twenty-first century observer, Pope Brock, wrote of the charlatan in his book *The Fraudulent Life of John Brinkley*: 'Though perhaps not the worst serial killer in American history, ranked by body count alone, he is at least a finalist for the crown.'

It is estimated that during his so-called medical career, Brinkley performed over 16,000 goat testicle transplants. Alongside his so-called sex-boosting surgery on men, he transplanted goat organs into women's abdomens near their ovaries, and performed transplants which he said could cure a whole host of conditions, ranging from insanity and acne to flu and high blood pressure. For £2,500, he would even implant human glands obtained from prisoners on Death Row.

The ease with which he established his reputation as a pioneering surgeon is astonishing, given that his procedures were simply the product of his own fertile imagination, harnessed so that he could make money out of gullible men. Brinkley was anything but a skilled surgeon or upstanding pillar of the community: he was a drunk who had bought the medical certificates that adorned his wall.

Previous occupations had included working as a snake-oil salesman in a road show and then establishing Greenville Electro Medical Doctors with a Chicago conman called James Crawford. In this business, the two men injected patients with coloured distilled water at £15 a shot to cure a variety of ills. When he set himself up as a surgeon, no one, it seemed, questioned the fact that Brinkley had failed to complete his training at medical schools – that themselves did not rate highly in the profession. Nor that he operated in unsterile conditions, often while under the influence of drink. Neither was there alarm at the high number of his patients' deaths.

Brinkley's surgical skills may have been sadly lacking but what he did possess was knowledge of certain experiments that were carried out in Europe in the late 1800s. One of the 'pioneers' of these was noted French physiologist Charles-Edouard Brown-Sequard, who had shocked the medical establishment by injecting himself with the crushed testicles of young dogs and guinea pigs. Afterwards, he claimed that he had regained the physical stamina and quick-thinking of his youth. Many men demanded what became known as *La Méthode Sequardienne*, but once the placebo effect wore off, all patients were left with was bitter disappointment.

Another French doctor, Serge Voronoff, was also causing controversy with his gland transplant experiments. Voronoff had worked as a doctor in the court of the King of Egypt, where he has spent a lot of time treating the court eunuchs who suffered from various illnesses. Voronoff claimed that maintaining active genital glands was the secret to good health. He said he had carried out experiments with an aging ram into which he had transplanted the testicles of a lamb. As a result, the older sheep's wool got thicker and he regained his sexual interest. Voronoff continued his work with the transplant of monkey testes into elderly men, claiming to have a high success rate.

Meanwhile, in the United States, Dr John Brinkley's reputation for his restorative goat-gland operations spread. This was helped by farmer Stittsworth who called round to see the 'doctor' a few weeks after his transplant. He wanted to thank Brinkley personally for his renewed libido. And then, when Stittsworth's wife gave birth to a baby boy – fittingly called Billy – Brinkley became known as the doctor who could help any farmer sow his wild oats, scatter his seeds and generally lead a very satisfying existence.

Brinkley's transplants did sometimes cause him problems. There was a period when he decided to use Angora goat testicles instead of those from the more common Toggenberg goat. Recipients were not happy – especially when Brinkley himself said they 'reeked like a steamy barn in midsummer'. In a bid to regain some of his 'credibility', Brinkley travelled to Californian where he performed a transplant on Harry Chandler, owner of the *Los Angeles Times*. Brinkley's career would have been in tatters had the operation gone wrong but, luckily for him, Chandler lived to tell the tale, rewarding the doctor with a great deal of excellent publicity.

It was during his visit to California that Brinkley realised radio was an effective medium through which to boost his reputation even further. So in 1923 he started up his own radio station, KFKB (Kansas First, Kansas Best), blasting out from Milford, Kansas, at 1,000 watts – amazingly powerful for the time. The station broadcast music, mainly to give listeners a break from the non-stop commercials but inadvertently bringing Country and Western to the masses. It also put out political programmes, Brinkley's own lectures on his field of medicine, and the innovative programme *Medical Question Box* during which he answered listeners' health queries. This latter slot was so successful that eight assistants had to be taken on to deal with the avalanche of mail.

Brinkley's intentions were far from altruistic, however. His advice was amateurish, incorrect and sometimes just plain silly. Above all, it normally included issuing a prescription accompanied by a designated number. These prescriptions could be filled at a local pharmacy – ones which were affiliated to the National Dr Brinkley Pharmaceutical Association which Brinkley had set up in collusion with pharmacists, who had no qualms about selling coloured water at ridiculously high prices.

Kickbacks from this business, together with Brinkley's highly lucrative transplant operations, made him an incredibly rich man. Some reports say that between 1933 and 1938, he earned around $12 million. At the height of his success, he owned three yachts (one reportedly used by the Duke and Duchess of Windsor for their honeymoon), a fleet of Cadillacs, airplanes, a vast mansion with his name picked out in the garden in flashing neon lights, and a two-storey pipe organ, which Brinkley would call a man from a Chinese theatre to come and play. Brinkley's bad taste went even further: he showed his admiration for Hitler by tiling his swimming pool with miniature swastikas.

What Brinkley could not buy was the respect and admiration of the legitimate medical world. And the greater his reputation, the more attention he attracted. In 1928, Morris Fishbein, editor of the *Journal of the American Medical Association*, called Brinkley a smooth-tongued charlatan and urged the authorities to take away his licence to practice medicine. He said all Brinkley's claims were no more than quackery. In response, Brinkley called the American Medical Association a 'meat-cutters union' and said its members were just jealous of him because he was taking their business.

The conflict got dirtier. The *Kansas City Star*, which owned a rival radio station, ran a series of damning reports on Brinkley, and in 1930 his medical licence was revoked by the Kansas State Medical Board after 43 deaths were attributed to his dubious 'cures'. Under pressure from the American Medical Association, the board found Brinkley guilty of 'immorality and unprofessional conduct'. That same year, the Federal Radio Commission refused to renew Brinkley's

KFKB broadcasting licence on the grounds that it was being used to promote fraud.

Brinkley hit back by campaigning for Governor of Kansas, a position which would have enabled him to appoint his own members to the medical board – ones who would give him his medical licence back. Despite promising to cure nearly every disease known to man and to build free clinics for the people, thus gaining the support of many ordinary folk, Brinkley polled only 30 per cent of the votes.

In 1931, he obtained a licence from the Government of Mexico to construct another powerful station on the AM dial, which was radiated by a 'sky wave antenna' held aloft by 300-ft towers. His station at Villa Acuña, Coahuila, was located on the other side of the Rio Grande from Del Rio, Texas. Under the call sign XER, Brinkley used his new border blasting facility to once more campaign for Governor. But despite broadcasts being heard in Kansas and as far north as Canada, Brinkley's attempt at being elected Governor failed again. Yet a third attempt ended in failure in 1934.

Meanwhile, Brinkley resumed his nefarious medical practices. Male radio listeners were offered an array of expensive concoctions which included injections and pills to increase their virility. Brinkley was also open to walk-in patients, having set up a new practice in the Roswell Hotel, Del Rio. Now he was performing prostate operations.

Brinkley next obtained a licence for another, yet more powerful Mexican station under the call letters XERA. When it signed on, its huge new high-gain antenna sent clear signals across Canada and the North Pole and into Russia. It was claimed that many Russians tuned to XERA and that the KGB used it to teach their spies English.

When World War Two started in Europe, Brinkley allowed his radio station to give a voice to Nazi sympathisers. This caused an outcry throughout America and in April 1941, the Mexican Government made a deal with the United States to curb renegade stations such as XERA. Brinkley was switched off the airwaves. His days as a powerful voice in the world of medicine were numbered.

He lost a libel suit against Dr Fishbein when his bogus qualifications and lack of medical knowledge were exposed in court. Then some of his patients sued him for malpractice. The Internal Revenue Service focussed on his high earnings and lack of tax payments, and he was indicted for mail fraud by the United States Postal Service. On January 26, 1942, he was forced to declare bankruptcy.

Brinkley might have pretended to work miracles on others but when it came to his own health, he was unable to perform any magic at all. He suffered a heart attack, then developed a blood clot and had to have his leg amputated. Bed-ridden but believing himself to be on the road to recovery, he turned his thoughts to religion and declared an ambition to become a famous preacher. The side of right intervened and the quack doctor never got his wish. He died on May 26, 1942, in San Antonio, Texas, and was buried in Memphis, Tennessee.

Brinkley's last words were reportedly: 'If Dr Fishbein goes to heaven, I want to go the other way.' That wish was almost certainly granted.

CHAPTER 5

Politician who 'Drowned' in Debt

At last they had their man. Britain's runaway aristocrat Lord Lucan was 'alive and well and living in Australia'. Lucan was wanted for murdering his children's nanny back in London and, until Christmas Eve 1974, had eluded capture.

Well, Interpol had it half right. The man they found was wanted. But he was not Lucan. He was British MP and former Labour Minister John Stonehouse who, faced with charges for fraud, had faked his death on Miami Beach just a month before. Now he had been discovered and one of the most audacious deceptions of the twentieth century was unravelling.

Stonehouse was a Labour Member of the British Parliament with great personal debts. His business empire lay in tatters and his personal life – he was attempting to keep both a wife and mistress in tow – was a constant strain. His attempt to drag himself out of the mire by apparently vanishing off the face of the earth was nothing short of a gigantic political scandal.

John Thomson Stonehouse was born into a left-wing political family on July 28, 1925. His father was secretary of the local trade union branch and his mother the president of the Southampton Co-operative Society. Stonehouse went to school in Southampton and Taunton and joined the Labour Party when he was sixteen. He went on to study at the London School of Economics and after holding a clerical position in the probation service, he launched himself into a career as an economist. Stonehouse became involved in co-operative enterprise, managing African Co-operative societies in Uganda between 1952 and 1954. From 1956 to 1962, he was a director of the London Co-operative Society and president from 1962 to 1964. In 1959, Stonehouse was expelled from Rhodesia for a speech in which he urged blacks to 'lift your heads high and behave as though the country belongs to you'. His efforts to highlight the independence of Bangladesh led to an offer of citizenship when the new state was declared in 1971.

Stonehouse was first elected as Labour Co-operative Member of Parliament for Wednesbury in a 1957 by-election. He had attempted to win seats in Parliament, first in Twickenham in 1950, then in Burton the following year, but lost on both occasions. As he took his seat in the House of Commons in 1957, Stonehouse seemed destined for the very top. After serving an apprenticeship on the back benches, he was talent-spotted by Labour leader Harold Wilson and put on the fast track to promotion, rising from junior Minister for Aviation to Technology Minister and then to Postmaster General.

As a Privy Counsellor, he was entitled to be known as the Right Honourable John Stonehouse. And he was so close to the Prime Minister that Wilson loaned him his private holiday home on the Isles of Scilly. He was even tipped as the PM's successor. Not one for modesty, Stonehouse declared to colleagues that his life plan was straightforward: become a millionaire and then Prime Minister. But by now, Stonehouse's arrogant manner was losing him favour with the Wilson administrations, and when the Labour Party was surprisingly defeated by the Conservatives in 1970, he was not appointed to a position in the Shadow Cabinet.

Stonehouse decided he could accept neither the comparative anonymity nor the reduced salary of life on the Commons back-benches. In an attempt to secure a regular income and ultimately makes his fortune, he began pumping money into a web of companies, including a merchant bank. Over the next four years, not one of them returned a decent profit. Stonehouse resorted to the oldest trick in the book – switching funds between them to satisfy investors and auditors that all was well. His heavily indebted business empire stretched to 23 separate companies.

In his heart, he probably knew it couldn't last, and in early 1974 he got wind that Department of Trade investigators were taking an interest in his companies. Even the political 'old boy' network couldn't help him now and he resolved to take desperate measures in a bid to avoid exposure. He disliked the idea of spending the rest of his life on the run so there was only one thing for it... he would have to 'die'.

Stonehouse decided that only one person should share his secret: his divorced mistress and secretary Sheila Buckley, then 28. The aim would be for them to move to New Zealand, living off whatever money he could smuggle out from the wreckage of his businesses. At that time, Stonehouse had debts of more than £800,000 after an attempt to set up a new investment bank in Bangladesh. He had also taken out a £170,000 insurance policy on his own life.

There was only one snag: he had to have a new identity. To get round this, Stonehouse used a technique described by thriller writer Frederick Forsyth in his classic *The Day of the Jackal*. He first tricked a hospital in his Walsall, Staffordshire, constituency to release personal details on two men of his own age who had died recently: Donald Mildoon and Joseph Markham. The 48-year-old MP then obtained copies of their birth certificates and, believing Markham's background was closest to his own, applied for a passport in that man's name. He obtained photo-booth shots of himself wearing glasses and smiling and on the back forged the counter-signature of an MP he knew to be dying of cancer, Neil McBride. The application was rubber-stamped at the Passport Office on August 2, 1974, and Stonehouse picked up his new passport. He now had a dual identity and could switch his name whenever necessary.

Then came the second part of his plan. Over the next three months, he opened 27 accounts in his own name and a further nine in the names of Markham or Mildoon. A Swiss bank received one huge cheque credited to Mr Markham while further amounts were quietly channelled via a London account to the Bank of New South Wales. Numerous credit cards were set up in Markham's name using an anonymous address at a downmarket London hotel. He even set up a company to help his cover story: 'J. A. Markham, export-import consultant'. The only exports it handled were cash and the only customer was Stonehouse.

After a dummy run to America, Stonehouse was ready for the real thing. He left London for Miami on November 19, 1974, with Jim Charlton, deputy chairman of one of his companies. The very next day, Stonehouse was assumed dead, a pile of clothes on Miami Beach testament to the suicide of a desperate man.

His 'death' shocked friends, family and colleagues – and also Mrs Helen Fleming, the 65-year-old receptionist on duty at the beachside office of the luxurious Fontainebleau Hotel. She would long remember the English gentleman who had strolled casually up to her booth on Miami Beach. Which was precisely his plan; before bidding Mrs Fleming farewell, the stranger passed the time of day with her and the pair enjoyed a long, uninterrupted chat. He mentioned that his name was John Stonehouse and that he was going for a swim. He wished her good day and she watched as he strolled casually down to the thundering surf, seemingly just another Briton soaking up the Florida sun. Hours later his clothes were found in a neat pile on the sand. Of John Stonehouse there was no trace.

When he failed to return from his swimming trip the following day, there seemed little doubt that he had drowned. The message flashed from Miami Beach Police Department to New Scotland Yard read: 'John Stonehouse Presumed Dead'. Of course, they were wrong. And the FBI was not convinced. They believed it highly unlikely that a man would drown at that stretch of the coast without a body being washed ashore. It was even suspected that the Mafia had been involved and a car park was excavated in the search for Stonehouse's remains. A body was found but it was not that of John Stonehouse.

In fact, the body of Stonehouse could not be found because he was very much alive. After dumping his clothes, the MP had raced up the beach to a ramshackle building where he had hidden a suitcase containing new clothes, cash and false identity papers. He took a taxi to the airport, flew to Hawaii via San Francisco and then called Sheila Buckley to tell her their scheme had worked like a dream. His optimism was premature, however.

Stonehouse arrived in Australia and was soon switching cash from a bank account in Melbourne, held under the name of

Mildoon, to one in New Zealand belonging to Joseph Markham. The amounts were more than enough to raise the suspicions of bank officials and soon the police were called in. A tail was put on Stonehouse who, by December 10, was transferring funds between a string of banks on a daily basis. The only brief respite came with a flight to Copenhagen for a tryst with Sheila Buckley. She had asked him to take her back with him but he had said it was too soon and would arouse suspicion. He travelled back from Denmark via Lebanon to Melbourne.

By now, the net seemed to be closing. Stonehouse had also attracted the attention of Australian immigration officials acting on information from overseas and was now under surveillance. Yet he might still have bluffed his way out had it not been for an unfortunate twist of fate. That autumn police across Australia had been briefed to look out for Lord Lucan. When Victoria State Police asked Scotland Yard for more pictures of Lucan they received some of John Stonehouse too. The missing MP bore a remarkable resemblance to Joseph Markham.

Stonehouse was arrested when police pounced on his luxury flat at the seaside resort of St Kilda on Christmas Eve 1974. He at first laughed off the questions about his false identity but a love note from Sheila Buckley found in his jacket ended the pretence. It read: 'Dear Dum Dums (her pet nickname for her lover). Do miss you. So lonely. Shall wait forever for you.'

Both Sheila and Stonehouse's 45-year-old wife Barbara flew to Australia to be at his side. Barbara, married to the MP for 24 years was initially elated that her husband had been found alive. But learning of Sheila Buckley's existence, she quickly returned to the UK to file divorce papers. Sheila stayed on until his extradition in June 1975 – the great delay caused partly by reluctance on the part of the Australians to deport a British MP. He had also tried to obtain offers of asylum from Sweden or Mauritius.

The case of the 'back from the dead' MP caused a sensation in Fleet Street. The *Daily Express* put 22 reporters on the story, including its cricket correspondent. The *News of the World* dispatched nine journalists, along with £15,000 in cash to buy

Stonehouse's story, and *The Times* asked its Sydney-based opera writer to get on the trail of him.

On his return to Britain, Stonehouse was remanded in Brixton Prison until August. During this time he began to process applying for the Chiltern Hundreds, one of two ways in which a British MP can resign, but he had a change of heart and did not sign the papers. He finally agreed to resign on August 28, 1976, as MP and also Privy Counsellor (becoming one of only three people to resign from the Privy Council in the twentieth century). By then, Stonehouse held the balance of power in Britain and his resignation put the Labour government, then headed by James Callaghan, in a minority with 315 seats compared to the 316 held by opposition parties. The by-election was won by Conservative Robin Hodgson.

Stonehouse appeared in court on 21 charges of fraud, theft, forgery, conspiracy to defraud, causing a false police investigation and wasting police time. He conducted his own defence but, after a 68-day trial, the disgraced politician was found guilty on eighteen counts of theft, forgery and fraud. He was given a seven-year sentence. Sheila Buckley got two years, suspended, for aiding and abetting him. The judge's comments at the end of the trial, that Stonehouse was an 'extremely persuasive, deceitful and ambitious man', failed to deter Sheila Buckley. She waited for him for three years – through three heart attacks suffered in prison and consequent open-heart surgery – to take back a bankrupt and seriously ill man.

Stonehouse was released early from prison in 1979. For several years, he worked as a volunteer fundraiser for an east London charity, Community Links. He joined the Social Democratic Party, which later merged to become the Liberal Democrats. Buckley and Stonehouse married in secret in 1981 and, for the next few years, the MP tried his hand in the world of publishing by becoming a thriller writer. He didn't make it big as an author. Perhaps his imagination couldn't compete with the astonishing exploits of the real John Stonehouse. He died, aged 62, in 1988. Sheila said of him: 'I've never met a man like him. John was gentle with everybody and, in particular, with me. I'll miss him forever.'

In December 2005, previously unseen documents released from the National Archives under the 30-year rule revealed how British diplomats working for Harold Wilson's government obtained a confidential psychiatric report on Stonehouse as he fought extradition. It had been submitted to the Australian authorities to support his claim that he had suffered a mental breakdown. A summary of the profile was sent to James Callaghan in 1975 when he was still Foreign Secretary, together with the warning from an unnamed official: 'It is clearly important that Mr Stonehouse should not find out that we have been given an account of the contents of this report.'

There was good reason for this. For the summary also revealed that Stonehouse was a Jekyll and Hyde character who had been posing as Joseph Markham for months prior to his disappearance to provide relief from the role of MP that he had come to hate. The summary stated: 'He believed he was ruined and evolved a bizarre scheme in 1974 to adopt a new identity. He spent short periods posing as Mr Markham, a private and honest individual, which apparently led to reduced tension. He began to dislike the personality of Stonehouse and therefore devised his plan to escape.'

There were further insights into Stonehouse's character. The report went on: 'The psychiatrist's opinion was that, as a child, Mr Stonehouse was anxious and withdrawn, though undoubtedly gifted. He achieved success as a young adult but at the expense of personal strain and repression of his emotional needs and his ability to communicate his true feelings. In middle age, stresses in his career led to a degree of disillusionment with himself. Mr Stonehouse suffered significant but "atypical depression". He thought of suicide but, deciding this was not the answer, devised a "suicide equivalent" – his disappearance from a beach in Miami.'

Stonehouse himself had quickly set about constructing a defence for his crimes, claiming he had been facing blackmail from South African business partners and had suffered a 'brainstorm' in Miami. In a memo sent to the Foreign Office and seen by Harold Wilson in Downing Street, Stonehouse said: 'My wish was to be released from the incredible pressures being put on me, particularly in my business activities and various attempts at blackmail. I considered, clearly wrongly, that the best action I could take was to create a new identity and attempt to live a new life away from these pressures. I suppose this can be summed up as brainstorm or a mental breakdown.'

The archive documents also included a rambling eighteen-page submission sent by Stonehouse to the Queen in his role as Privy Counsellor, protesting his innocence – with a note from one official advising that it be ignored – and a series of memos sent to senior Labour Party figures insisting he was the victim of wide-ranging conspiracy. They included a polemic against the press; in a letter to the then Leader of the Commons, Ted Short, Stonehouse blamed Fleet Street for his downfall saying: 'Press freedom is a false god to worship; it has become a weapon in the hands of callow, cynical and completely irresponsible men who delight in undermining and destroying active people in politics and business who are the constructive and positive elements in society. This negativism of much contemporary journalism is a cancer in the body politic and is gradually eating away at the vitals of British democracy.'

It was, of course, Stonehouse himself who brought about his political demise. He was a coward who believed the only way out from punishment for fraud, and fall from grace, was to 'die'.

CHAPTER 6

'Colonel' who Fleeced 'The King'

Colonel Tom Parker, the cigar-chomping manager who catapulted Elvis Presley to mega-stardom, was still working when he suffered a sudden stroke and died in 1997, at the age of 87. He was the consultant on a projected Elvis movie and was advisor to the Hilton hotel chain on entertainment. His weeping wife Lois was at his Las Vegas bedside and tributes from many of the gambling city's luminaries were mentioned when he was cremated and interred at Palm Cemetery on Eastern Avenue.

'He was a generous and caring human being,' said a Hilton executive who met him daily as he wandered from business meetings onto the gaming floor. 'He loved to play slot machines. He would say, "I'm going down to get my exercise"!'

The ageing rock manager was a gambler, that much is true – an inveterate gambling addict and big-time loser. But 'generous and caring' he was not. He was a grasping phoney who milked the Presley money-making machine for multi-millions. He was not a 'colonel' in any US Army sense. He was not even American. And his name was not Tom Parker.

Evidence that arose after his death indicated that he may even have been a murderer on the run all his conniving life. According to his biographer, American journalist Alanna Nash, in his youth he may have bludgeoned a young woman to death.

When his name first came to public notice in America, Parker lied about his childhood, claiming to have been born in Huntington, West Virginia, and to have run away at an early age to join a circus owned by an uncle. In the late twenties, he had been almost a hobo, working at fairgrounds, before joining the Army for a four-year spell, during which he was shipped out to Hawaii. He was accused of desertion and discharged in

1933 because of mental illness described as 'a constitutional psychopathic state'.

After leaving the US Army, he pretty well disappeared back into the travelling carnivals that criss-crossed the Southern states – a hustler looking for a way to make a living. The best-known story about him at this time was his supposed invention of a faked 'dancing chicken' act – where the poor birds hopped around on a tin tray with an electric current running through it. The story was later disputed by his widow Lois, who said: 'To set the record straight, there were never any "dancing chickens". This was a joke the Colonel used to test the gullibility of people. It has been repeated (and believed) so many times that there is no doubt people are gullible!'

However, his talents with animals were recognised elsewhere. He was once employed washing circus elephants, he painted sparrows yellow and sold them as canaries, and he was a town dog catcher and pet cemetery proprietor in Florida.

Eventually, his luck turned and, despite being tone deaf, he moved into the Country and Western scene. In 1939 he became manager of Gene Austin and travelled with Gene's 'Models & Melodies' show. As Country and Western became a musical force to be reckoned with, he set up on his own, booking country acts. In 1944 he became manager of Eddy Arnold, who three years later topped the country charts for 53 weeks in a row.

During this period, he began labelling himself 'Colonel', having been given the honorary title by at least one Southern governor. In 1955 Parker became personal manager to singer Hank Snow and booked young upcoming singers as opening acts on Hank's shows. That was the year he heard about a boy of 19 who lived in Memphis. He put him on stage on a Hank Snow show – and Elvis Presley's stellar career path (that ended with him being tagged as simply 'The King') was under way.

Elvis was managed by Bob Neal at the time but, as Presley's 'special advisor', Parker negotiated a recording contract with RCA Victor – insisting that the young singer choose his own songs – an unheard-of concession at the time. Parker was rewarded by becoming Elvis' personal manager in 1956 and, by the end of their first year together, the *Wall Street Journal* reported that, since the Colonel began marketing Elvis merchandise, they had grossed some $22 million in sales. Musical history was being made and, whatever one may think of Parker's ethics, no one can deny that he worked night and day for his artist.

As a promoter, Parker was inspired. His years on the fairgrounds had taught him how to persuade people to do what he wanted. The negotiating skills he'd learned worked wonderfully when doing deals for Elvis – and the personal deals for himself that Elvis never knew about. But his manner put many off. Elvis's beloved mother didn't trust him from the start and undoubtedly voiced her reservations most forcefully to her doting son. Elvis heeded her in almost every sphere but Parker somehow had a hold on Presley that kept him in thrall for the whole of his life. 'It's better to be feared than liked,' was his proud motto.

The phoney Colonel never imagined Elvis' success could last, openly mocking some of his million-selling records. So he set out to seize what he could while the dollars were rolling in, fleecing Elvis of up to 50 per cent of his income and adding untold 'expenses' on top of that.

As he steered Elvis into movies, he so upset studio bosses that many refused to speak to him. Those that did had to bow to his personal demands. For instance, Parker never paid for office space but added it to every contract. One studio found this so unprofessional that they placed him in the men's room, with a sign on the door: 'Colonel Parker's West Coast Office'. Two studio executives who had to do business with him found Parker sitting on the lavatory, trousers around his ankles, while his 'secretary' sat on a stool in the shower.

Suspicions about Parker first arose in 1958 when Elvis was drafted into the Army and sent to Germany. Elvis's grandmother, father and several friends accompanied him. But the Colonel stayed behind. Why? And why later, when so many lucrative offers were coming in from around the world, did Parker never take Presley on tour abroad?

The reason was that Tom Parker was an illegal immigrant and feared that if he ever left the United States he would not be allowed back in. Further, as a non-citizen, he would not have been able to acquire a US passport and, if he filed an application, might have been deported.

His real place of birth was Breda, in the Netherlands, where he was born in 1909 and christened Andreas Comelis, the fifth child of Adam and Maria van Kuijk, a devout Roman Catholic couple. At 16, Andreas, who was nicknamed by his family as 'Dries', began working on the ships which sailed out of Rotterdam. Then, in 1929, with no word to his family, he disappeared, leaving behind his Bible, his personal papers, his pay-packet, his savings and even his clothes. For a few years he sent his family postcards but once they stopped, they did not hear from him again for three decades.

Alanna Nash, the American journalist who wrote his biography – *The Colonel: The Extraordinary Story of Colonel Tom Parker And Elvis Presley*, published by Aurum Books in 2003 – believes he may have come up with the answer. By assiduously researching police and court archives/newspaper records and with the help of Dutch journalists, Nash has linked Parker with an unsolved murder. On the day Andreas disappeared, a young housewife named Anna van den Enden was found bludgeoned to death in her husband's greengrocers shop, not far from the van Kuijks' home. Andreas would have known her; he would have visited the shop and they would have attended the same church.

Nash interviewed former Presley associates who believed the manager was capable of such a crime. Lamar Fike, an aide who rowed frequently with Parker over the manager's neglect of the star, told her: 'I don't think there's any doubt he killed that woman. He had a terrible temper. He and I got into some violent, violent fights.' Parker's employee, Byron Raphael, said: 'He had a terrible temper and a terrible mean streak. It took very little to set him off. In those fits of rage, he was a very dangerous man, and he certainly appeared capable of killing.' And Parker himself, explaining why he never drank, said alcohol changed his personality and made him 'act mean'.

Nash added: 'Nothing in the police report ever connected van Kuijk to this still unsolved crime. But to say that his behaviour for the rest of his life was suspicious is an understatement.'

Was this the secret Parker was so careful to hide? The truth about his early years was revealed in 1960 when one of his sisters recognised her missing sibling in a magazine photograph of the middle-aged manager standing next to Elvis. The family made contact with him but he was apparently not keen to see them. A younger brother travelled to Hollywood to see him but Parker refused to return to Holland.

He was just too frightened to leave the United States. And although he could have made extra multi-millions by sending Presley on tour abroad, he wouldn't allow his star to travel either. Presley toured Canada in 1957, with concerts in Toronto, Ottawa and Vancouver, but at the time of these, crossing the US-Canada border did not require a passport.

Instead of encouraging his client to broaden his style, his appeal and indeed his outlook, Parker – who still believed Elvis's career was to be short-lived – greedily signed a string of Hollywood deals for 30 cheap and hastily produced movies. 'All Elvis' movies are good for is to make money,' Parker said. He wasn't interested in the subjects or the scripts, only that the songs in them be published by companies that he and his associates controlled.

The result was that after Elvis got out of the army in 1960, he tried to rebel against the songs and films he was being given. He hated performing them; he began despising himself. He began to hate the Colonel. Yet, from whatever sense of dependency, he stuck with him. And, as the Sixties rock-and-rolled on, Elvis's syrupy music was becoming a joke.

'Elvis was trapped by his dependency on the Colonel,' said Jerry Leiber, who co-wrote *Jailhouse Rock* and a dozen other hits. 'Presley worshipped Parker as his maker and saviour, but despised him because he was never able to take control of his own life'.

Then two dangerous addictions made an unpleasant situation critical. Parker became a gambling addict and Presley became hooked on drugs. The Colonel was losing a million dollars a year at one casino alone and couldn't afford to loosen the hold he had over his unhappy star.

Just how far they both had sunk is illustrated by the events in Louisville, Kentucky, in May 1977, as Elvis lay moaning incoherently on his hotel bed in a drugged stupour. His doctor was trying to revive him by splashing him with iced water when in walked his manager. Elvis's biographer reports that at least one nervous member of Presley's entourage believed that Parker, witnessing Presley's drug addiction at its worst, could no longer ignore it and would have him whisked off to hospital. Instead, the Colonel flew into a rage, screaming: 'The only thing that's important is that he's on that stage tonight. Nothing else matters.'

Three months later, Elvis was dead. A bloated, drug-sodden wreck, he was aged just 42. Parker, who had milked him of a $100 million fortune over the previous 22 years, immediately began marketing his death. He needed even more money to pay off his gambling debts – which Elvis himself had confided to a friend shortly before he died were an astonishing $8 million – half a million more than Elvis's entire estate. Twenty years later, when Parker died, he had gambled away even more of the fortune Elvis had brought him, leaving just $900,000.

'Colonel Tom Parker' had lost his vast fortune, along with his identity. Also lost in the web of mystery he had spun around himself over the years was the fate of his Dutch neighbour, Anna van den Enden.

CHAPTER 7

A Past Master at Deception

Even to the expert eye, it looked like a Monet. The colours and brushstrokes of *Morning on the Seine* were just perfect. But only the artist knew the truth.

And that artist was not a great Impressionist. He was a master forger. The 'Monet' had been painted in Dulux house paints.

For eight years, John Myatt, a former schoolteacher from Staffordshire, reproduced works of great art and presented them as original masterpieces. He even fabricated paintings by abstract artist Picasso that had never existed and drawings by impressionist Henri Matisse. All were passed off as genuine through Myatt's accomplice John Drewe, the work sold for thousands or pounds to galleries and private collectors.

So audacious was Myatt – described as perpetrating 'the biggest art fraud of the Twentieth Century' – that it was almost a shame when the painter had a brush with the law.

It was an international notoriety that was far removed from his humble beginnings. John Myatt was born in 1945, the son of God-fearing farmer Herbert and his wife Freda. He was always destined for an artistic future, first winning a choral scholarship to King's, the cathedral school in Worcester, then going on to study art at Staffordshire Art College.

'I had always liked drawing but I wasn't one of the best in the class,' Myatt was to confess later. 'I was more interested in music than painting.'

In fact, he worked as a songwriter for a while and even wrote a song, *Silly Games*, which was a UK Top 40 hit for a singer called Janet Kay in 1979. After making a life for himself in the music industry in London, Myatt then decided to return to Staffordshire where he married a local girl. The couple had two children, a girl born in 1983 and a boy born in 1985.

By this time, Myatt was teaching but gave it up when his wife left him and the children for another man. Being at home was not something Myatt was used to, and he needed to earn a living which fitted in with being a full-time parent. He decided to capitalise on a talent he had for mimicking other artists' styles, a knack he had discovered some years earlier while at art school.

At first, Myatt painted for his own amusement and for friends, and then tried to make a living by painting original works in the style of well-known artists. He placed an advertisement in the satirical magazine *Private Eye* which read 'Genuine fakes. Nineteen and Twentieth Century paintings from £150.'

Myatt was happy enough just to supply his honest fakes. But one man who answered the advert saw greater potential. John Drewe, a charismatic character who wore a mohair coat and drove an expensive Bristol car, commissioned some of Myatt's Great Masters fakes to decorate his London home.

After two years, Myatt was running out of ideas to copy and suggested painting a piece in the style of French Cubist Albert Gleizes – this was created like nearly all his 'reproductions' while his children slept upstairs. Without Myatt's knowledge, Drewe took the painting to London fine art auctioneers Christies, who valued it at £25,000. Myatt said he could never forget the day Drewe telephoned him and asked him: 'Are you sitting down?'

'He told me what he'd done and asked me how I'd like £12,500. I said I'd like it very much.' Unwittingly, that was the moment the honest, church-going lad from a farming background, became one of the art world's most artful crooks. He admitted later: 'It didn't take me long to make the decision. It was the same amount of money as I could earn in a year as a supply teacher. I squared it with my conscience, saying no one was getting hurt and I honestly thought it was a one-off.'

The painting had been done on the living room table of Myatt's home. He couldn't believe that something as unsophisticated as that could be deemed an original by the experts. Counting his good fortune on this slight fall from the honest life he had led, Myatt continued his job as a supply teacher two days a week. But it was hard not to take advantage of such a rewarding sideline.

Pictures in the style of masters like Roger Bissiere, Marc Chagall, Le Corbusier, Jean Dubuffet, Albert Giacometti, Mattise, British abstract artist Ben Nicholson, Nicholas de Stael and Graham Sutherland followed. At the time of his arrest, police estimated Myatt had painted 200 forgeries to a regular schedule, delivering them to Drewe in London.

The scam 'just grew' Myatt confessed. 'The problem was I didn't admit to myself it was criminal. It all seemed a bit unreal. John Drewe would just ask me to do paintings and I'd deliver them to him. He handled all the selling, passing them off as lost originals.'

Using all his powers of imagination, Drewe created suitably fake histories for the fake paintings, which he sold for an average of £30,000. He used art gallery notepaper and forged receipts, and he even made fake entries in the indexes of major galleries like the Tate and the Victoria and Albert Museum. Auctions houses Christie's, Philips and Sotheby's and dealers in London, Paris and New York were all the recipients of the forged works.

Cheekily, Drewe donated £20,000 to the Tate, leading officials to trust him as a 'serious researcher'.

By the mid-1900s, Myatt was finding it increasingly hard to reconcile his Christian faith with such gross dishonesty. He confided his fears to Drewe who agreed the scam would come to an end. The parting of the ways was acrimonious and Drewe is said to have threatened Myatt with a gun. It is not known whether Drewe actually continued his deception after this, but for a year Myatt believed his criminal life was behind him.

However, on September 25, 1995, the police called at his home. Just how they got onto him is unclear. Some say his ex-wife tipped them off. Others that a former girlfriend of Drewe found incriminating documents in a property the couple had shared. Myatt knew the game was up and quickly confessed. He offered to return £18,000 of his ill-gotten gains – and to help convict Drewe.

The trial took four years to come to court because Drewe kept jumping bail. Police had raided his Surrey gallery and found materials he had used to forge certificates of authenticity. Drewe had also altered provenances (the history and background of works of art) to genuine paintings to link them to Myatt's fakes.

Eventually, the trial against the two men opened at London's Southwark Crown Court in September 1998. It heard how some of the forgeries were aged with vacuum cleaner dust and mud. The works were created from ordinary household emulsion like Dulux and with coffee, to make the canvas look old, watered down with the lubricant KY Jelly.

The police, who had recovered only 60 of the forgeries, claimed the two men made at least a £1 million from the start of the scam in 1986 until they were arrested in 1994. The two men denied it was anything like this amount.

On February 12, 1999, Myatt was sentenced to a year in jail for conspiracy. He was released the following June, serving just four months of his sentence.

Despite his protestations of innocence, claiming 'a cesspit of festering corruption' in the art world had made him a 'scapegoat' to conceal 'international arms deals known to the government', Drewe was found guilty of conspiracy to defraud, two counts of forgery, one of theft and one of using a false instrument with intent. He was sentenced to six years and served two.

Judge Geoffrey Rivlin, QC, described the case as 'extraordinary'. He said Drewe had been the 'chief architect, organiser and driving force behind a massive fraud' and had demonstrated he was a 'highly imaginative master forger of documents'. One dealer called him a 'mad genius.'

Myatt was said by his defence counsel Stuart Denny to be 'deeply ashamed' of what he had done. Mr Denny said he had been manipulated at a time when he was short of money and vulnerable.

Myatt was indeed remorseful, saying: 'I was glad my parents were dead so they didn't have to suffer the humiliation, but I didn't feel any sense of relief. I would happily have taken my secret to the grave.'

He later admitted: 'I regret what I did and there's no excuse for it. At the time, I was a single parent going through a very rough patch and I seized on the opportunity. If the same offer were made to me now, I certainly wouldn't get involved.'

While serving his time in Brixton Prison, Myatt bided the time doing what he did best – painting and drawing. He drew pictures of prison warders and fellow inmates (using pencils and papers sent in to him by his arresting officer) in exchange for phone cards. When released, Myatt was commissioned by the same officer to paint his family's portrait. Other commissions followed from members of the prosecution team who wanted fake originals to adorn their chambers. Celebrities were among those who wanted to boast of having a Myatt in their collection.

Myatt had a ready-made career awaiting him. Something of a celebrity himself now, he was offered an exhibition called Genuine Fakes. Other exhibitions followed, with his work selling for up to £45,000 each.

'I'm painting in the style of the great artists so ordinary people can own beautiful artwork without having to spend millions,' he told a journalist. 'The great thing is, if you hate the picture you can say so without fear of ridicule because it isn't really by anyone famous. And I earn more money now.'

Each of Myatt's genuine fakes bears his name in indelible ink and some are even fitted with an identifying computer chip – in case they are ever passed off as the 'real thing'.

When not painting, Myatt leaves his barn conversion home in Staffordshire and travels the country giving lectures, along with a retired Scotland Yard policeman, on the history of art forgery. There was talk of a film being made of his eight-year forgery 'masterclass' with titles such as 'ArtCon' and 'Genuine Fakes' being suggested.

The man whom even police considered to be a loveable rogue was lucky enough to find happiness when he was married again, to Rosemary, a member of the local church choir for whom he was organist. They embarked on a contented life, walking their dog and returning to a home adorned with Myatt's work cheekily labelled F.A.K.E.

For a laugh, someone advertised 'Original John Myatts' for sale in *Private Eye*. But while Myatt came out of those criminal days relatively unscathed, there are still his victims to remember. More than 100 art collectors were cheated and 120 forgeries are still in circulation.

Said Myatt: 'Even if I could identify them, I wouldn't. What good would it do? If someone has paid a lot of money for something they think is an original, there is nothing to be gained by retrospectively disillusioning them.'

Having suffered badly at the hands of The Dulux Faker, various auction houses, the Tate and the Victoria and Albert Museum have revised their security arrangements. They are fully aware that, had Myatt and his accomplice Drew not been found out by chance, they could still be buying old masters created at the hands of a master forger.

CHAPTER 8

Captain of Köpenick

he discovery was too good an opportunity to miss. A humble cobbler had mastered the tone that army officers, whose boots he mended, barked orders at their low-ranking soldiers – and noted how the minions literally jumped to attention. Thus, through his skill at mimicry, lowly-born Wilhelm Voigt had created a starring role for himself. He would go on to be known forever as 'the Captain of Köpenick' for a hoax which made a laughing stock out of a platoon of German soldiers.

Friedrich Wilhelm Voigt was born in Tilsit, Prussia (now Sovetsk, Russia) in February 1849. He was destined never to lead an honest life, and at the age of 14 was sentenced to two weeks in prison for theft, which led to his expulsion from school. He learned the trade of shoe-making from his father, although this seemed no more than a stop-gap between his spells in prison. Between 1864 and 1891, Voigt was imprisoned several times for thefts and forgery, and upon leaving prison in February 1906, he became something of a hobo, drifting around the country until going to live with his sister in Rixdorf, near Berlin. There, Voigt worked briefly as a court shoe-maker until, in August 1906, he was expelled from Berlin as an undesirable. Officially, he left for Hamburg but actually remained in Berlin as an unregistered resident.

What prompted Voigt to embark on his notorious escapade we will never know, but in October that same year, he left his job at a shoe factory and went on a strange shopping expedition, purchasing items of second-hand Prussian officer uniforms from various shops until he had a complete 'officer's look'. Voigt spent an entire week's wages on the uniform and set about practising the arrogant walk of a Prussian officer as he roamed the streets of Berlin. Astonished at how impressive he looked, despite his bulging stomach, the moustachioed cobbler began to assume the role perfectly. He had learned to mimic the speech and mannerisms of officers while mending their boots as an apprentice; now he found that he could bark orders at passing soldiers and, for the first time in his life, he saw people leap to action when he addressed them.

The German awe of uniforms and the public's willingness to accept directions unquestioningly from anyone in authority gave Voigt the idea for his greatest scam. He donned the clothing, went to the local army barracks in the suburb of Plotzensee and ordered four passing grenadiers and a sergeant to come to him. 'Halt!' he imperiously told them. 'I am Captain Voigt and this unit is now under my command.' Voigt's orders were answered without hesitation. Realising the power he had over them, Voigt began to enjoy his role. He dismissed the sergeant, telling him to report to his superiors, and then commandeered six more soldiers from a shooting range.

That is how Wilhelm Voigt came to be marching through the streets of Berlin at the head of a platoon of soldiers. The men under his command didn't know what they were doing – but they never expected to be told anyway. So when they arrived at a station on the Berlin circular railway, they did not argue as their captain ordered them aboard a train for the town of Köpenick, a dozen or so miles away. He ushered the corporal and the privates into a workmen's carriage while he himself relaxed in a first-class compartment.

The train was bound for Köpenick but Voigt ordered his men to disembark at a stop five miles earlier. He reckoned it would be more impressive if he and his platoon marched into town. And so it was as, after two hours' march, the group arrived in the main street of Köpenick and halted outside the town hall he was later to 'occupy'. Voigt told local police to 'care for law and order', requesting that they prevent calls for one hour at the local post office.

Voigt then gave each of his men a mark and told them to find an eating place but to be back at the same spot within the hour. The nine men returned as ordered and Voigt placed two of them on guard outside the town hall while marching the rest inside and up the stairs. Arriving at the office of the mayor, Voigt burst in and announced to the startled dignitary: 'You are under arrest!'

'On what authority?' asked the mayor, Georg Langerhans. 'Where is your warrant?'

'My warrant is the men I command,' was Voigt's perfunctory response, as the phoney captain summoned in the borough treasurer and told him to open the safe. The official handed over the town's entire treasury of 4,000 marks and was rewarded with an 'official' receipt – which Voigt signed in the name of one of his former jail directors. The mayor, his wife, the deputy mayor and the treasurer were then gathered together in the street under the guard of the nine soldiers. He told the group they were being arrested on suspicion of crooked accounting and that his men would be taking them to Berlin for interrogation.

Voigt then requisitioned three vehicles in which to remove his captives. One was a small cab, in which the captain deposited himself and the cash box. The soldiers and their prisoners filled the other two vehicles which, upon Voigt's orders, were driven off to a police station 15 miles away. And that, of course, was the last they saw of him, as Voigt roared off in a cloud of dust with his 4,000 marks. His first stop was Köpenick railway station where he had taken the precaution of depositing a change of civilian clothes. With his military disguise wrapped in a parcel under his arm, Voigt took a train back to Berlin, arriving at his lodging at roughly the same time that the soldiers and their prisoners arrived at the police station and waited for their captain ... and waited ... and waited.

The news of the confidence trick was flashed around the world. It was a pantomime that reflected badly on the impressionable nature of the German character and sorely tested the German sense of humour as the Prussian military became a laughing stock. However, the Kaiser, himself a Wilhelm, was reported to have roared with laughter when he heard of the stunt. He told an aide: 'Such a thing could only happen in Germany.' And the newspaper *Berliner Tageblat* said that the culprit, if found, should not be punished but rewarded for teaching the nation a lesson. The English found the whole thing particularly funny, seeing it as confirmation of the German stereotype.

A report in the October 26 issue of the *Illustrated London News* read: 'For years, the Kaiser has been instilling into his people reverence for the omnipotence of militarism, of which the holiest symbol is the German uniform. Offences against this fetish have incurred condign punishment. Officers who have not considered themselves saluted in due form have drawn their swords with impunity on offending privates.' In that same issue, writer G. K. Chesterton pointed out: 'The most absurd part of this absurd fraud (at least to English eyes) is one which, oddly enough, has received comparatively little comment. I mean the point at which the mayor asked for a warrant and the captain pointed to the bayonets of his soldiery and said "These are my authority". One would have thought anyone would have known that no soldier would talk like that.'

Although the German public seemed to be highly amused at Voigt's antics, the German army and the Berlin police force instituted a high-priority investigation. Ten days after his visit to Köpenick, Voigt was arrested in a dawn raid on his slum room, where he was quietly drinking a cup of coffee with about half of his ill-gotten gains still stuffed in his pocket; the rest had been spent. He was allowed to finish his breakfast while detectives removed the bundle of military clothing from under his bed. Marched to the police station, the now-famous crook was feted and given a bottle of port.

Voigt's trial in December 1906 was a sensation. More than 10,000 people applied for entry to the court to see him tried for forgery, impersonating an officer and wrongful imprisonment. The judge's penalty of four years' imprisonment was deemed harsh by many – including the Kaiser who, in an unprecedented intervention, pardoned him half way through the sentence. He was released in 1908 and discovered that a play had been written about his exploits, titled *The Captain of Köpenick*. He asked for and received free seats for all his jailbird friends. He also signed photographs of himself as 'Captain of Köpenick'.

Voigt's wax figure appeared in the wax museum of Unter den Linden four days after his release from prison. He appeared at the museum to sign pictures but public officials threw him out. Voigt's wax image later appeared at London's famous Madame Tussaud's. Despite being ordered to keep a low profile, Voigt toured Dresden, Vienna and Budapest in variety shows, restaurants and amusement parks. In 1909, he published a book about his hoax. A planned tour of America nearly didn't come off because the immigration authorities refused to give him a visa, but he turned up there anyway via Canada.

Allotted a small pension by a rich German dowager with a fine sense of humour, Voigt moved to Luxembourg in 1910 and supplemented his income by working as a waiter and shoe-maker. Two years later he bought a house and retired, but First World War inflation reduced his wealth, and not even the dowager's pension kept him afloat.

Voigt died in Luxembourg in January 1922. But his notoriety as a Prussian prankster who had sorely tested the German sense of humour was to be further immortalised. In 1931, German author Carl Zuckmayer wrote a play, *The Captain of Köpenick*, and films were made about Voigt's exploits. British playwright John Mortimer wrote and adapted a production from the earlier German play, which was performed by the National Theatre Company at the Old Vic on March 9, 1971. The shoemaker who had masqueraded as the Hauptman von Köpenick would have been more than satisfied to see just how far his own play-acting had taken him.

CHAPTER 9

Clone 'Genius' Accused

It is the stuff science-fiction fantasies are made of – the creation of identical human beings in a laboratory. Once, this would indeed have been something imagined in a future far off. But the Twenty First century saw it becoming a reality.

It was therefore a tragedy that one man, desperate to be the first in the pioneering world of cloning, allowed fiction to cloud fact. Instead of being hailed as the most successful cloner of modern times, South Korean scientist Professor Hwang Woo-suk was forced to resign in disgrace after much of his data was revealed as fake. There were also the ethical issues to contend with – of using donor eggs from staff, paying for women to donate them and issuing false information. Above all, there were the charges of embezzlement of billions of pounds.

It was public humiliation and the end of an illustrious career for a man who had the potential to create carbon copy human embryos and cure life-threatening diseases.

Hwang's start in life was humble. He was born on January 29, 1953, in Bu-yeo, South Korean's Chungnam province, during the Korean War and worked at a farm to finance his studies. Hwang's father died when he was only five, leaving his mother to bring up six children on her own. Hwang attended Daejeon High School and then went on to study at the prestigious Seoul National University.

Despite his professors urging him to become a medical doctor, Hwang chose to be a vet instead. After earning his doctorate, he briefly practiced veterinary medicine, before moving into the field of scientific research. Combining his veterinary and scientific knowledge, his aim was to create a genetically superior Korean cow.

Eventually, Hwang became a full-time researcher at Seoul National University and was obsessed with his work. He would turn up at the laboratory at 6am each day and leave at midnight, only ever seeing his wife briefly. As he stated himself: 'I work all day long. It is my habit and hobby. I am driven by the quest to find cures for the incurable.' Hwang once remarked that he and his team's weekly work schedule consists of 'Monday-Tuesday-Wednesday-Thursday-Friday-Friday-Friday'.

It was no wonder that the marriage of a man so driven would fail. In 1988 Hwang divorced the woman who had borne him two sons. It was a traumatic time for him as he was also being treated for liver cancer. Formerly a Roman Catholic, Hwang now sought solace in Buddhism to the extent that he told friends that if he had not become a scientist, he would have been a Buddhist monk. Hwang married again in 1997.

Hwang first found the attention he sought in February 1999, when he announced that he had created a cloned dairy cow called Yeongrong-I. Already, the seeds of doubt were there. Hwang willingly allowed interviews and photo-calls but failed to provide scientifically verifiable data for his research. His next claim came only two months later, in April 1999, when he announced the cloning of a Korean cow, Jin-I, but again without providing any verifiable data.

Hwang continued his research in creating genetically-modified livestock, including cows and pigs, at one time claiming to have created a BSE-resistant cow – again not verified. There was also the promise to clone a Siberian tiger.

In February 2004, Hwang and his team announced that they had successfully created a cloned human embryo, an embryonic stem cell, through a procedure called the somatic cell nuclear transfer method, and they published their paper in the March 12 issue of the journal *Science*. Although already established as an expert in animal cloning and enjoying celebrity status in South Korea, Hwang now really hit the headlines – because this was the first reported success in human somatic cell cloning. Until Hwang's claim, it was generally agreed that creating a human stem cell by cloning was next to impossible due to the complexity of primates. Hwang explained that his team used 242 eggs to create a single cell line.

But by now, some ethical doubts about the research practices within Hwang's team were being raised. *Nature* magazine published a claim that work had been conducted using egg cells that had been donated by a junior researcher. Many ethical concerns surround donation by research group members, due to the possibility that junior members may be coerced or pressurised into the process by senior researchers.

Nevertheless, *Time* magazine named Hwang one of its 'People Who Mattered in 2004', stating that Hwang 'has already proved that human cloning is no longer science fiction, but a fact of life'.

Hwang announced an even greater achievement a year later in May 2005, with the claims that he and his team had created eleven human embryonic stem cells using 185 eggs. His work, published in the June 17 issue of *Science*, was instantly hailed as a breakthrough in biotechnology, because the cells were allegedly created with somatic cells from patients of different age and gender, while the stem cell of 2004 was created with eggs and somatic cells from a single female donor.

The main aim of such research as Hwang Woo-suk's is to successfully clone a human embryo, produce stem cells from it and create a technique that could one day provide cures for a range of diseases. Woo-suk's latest success meant every patient could receive custom-made treatment with no immune reactions. In addition, Hwang's claim meant that his team had boosted their success rate by fourteen times and that this technology could be medically viable.

Hwang made further headlines in May 2005 when he criticised US President George W. Bush's policy on embryonic stem cell research. Following on from his apparent earlier success, Hwang announced on August 3, 2005, that his team of researchers had become the first team to successfully clone a dog, an Afghan hound named Snuppy.

Shortly after all this ground-breaking work, Hwang was appointed to head the new World Stem Cell Hub, a facility that was to be the world's leading stem cell research centre. By the end of the year, however, his status would be tarnished.

On November 21, following an intense media probe, Roh Sung-il, one of Hwang's close collaborators and head of MizMedi Women's Hospital, held a news conference during which he admitted he had paid women £700 each for donating their eggs (which were later used in Hwang's research). Roh claimed Hwang was unaware of this, while the South Korean Ministry of Health assured that no laws or ethical guidelines had been breached as there were no commercial interests involved in this payout.

But Hwang's integrity was put in doubt when it was revealed that a news programme, *PD Su-cheop*, had scheduled a follow-up report questioning his achievement published in *Science* magazine in June 2005. This caused a furious backlash among ordinary South Koreans, and the reaction only intensified when it was discovered that Kim Sun-Jong, one of Hwang's researchers from MizMedi, was coerced by illegal means to testify against Hwang. As a result, the scheduled broadcast was cancelled and the network even made a public apology to the nation. The general opinion was that the show was at fault and not Hwang. But this did not stop other journalists probing into Hwang's claims.

Close scrutiny revealed that several of the photos of purportedly different cells were in fact photos of the same cell. Hwang responded that these additional photos were accidentally included and that there was no such duplication in the original submission to *Science*. This was later confirmed by the journal. Researchers also raised questions about striking similarities between the DNA profiles of the cloned cells.

Then in November 2005, Gerald Schatten, a University of Pittsburgh researcher who had worked with Hwang for two years, asked *Science* to remove his name from the paper, giving as a reason that there were 'allegations from someone involved with the experiments that certain elements of the report may be fabricated'. In an interview, Schatten said: 'My decision is grounded solely on concerns regarding oocyte (egg) donations in Hwang's research reported in 2004.'

Meanwhile, several prominent scientists, including British embryologist Sir Ian Wilmut, who cloned Dolly the sheep in 1996, and Bob Lanza, a cloning expert based in Worcester, Massachusetts, called on Hwang to submit his paper to an outside group for independent analysis – essentially, the same test used to determie parenthood for children of questionable legitimacy. Lanza noted: 'You can't fake the results if they're carried out by an independent group. I think this simple test could put the charges to rest.'

Hwang failed to accept the challenge. As public opinion began to turn against him, he maintained a low profile and was then hospitalised for alleged stress-related fatigue. On November 24, he held a press conference in Seoul, in which he declared his intention of resigning from most of his official posts. He also apologised for some of his actions, saying: 'I was blinded by work and my drive for achievement.'

He denied coercing two of his researchers into donating eggs but admitted that, when he discovered they had done so without his knowledge, he had continued to issue denials. He said he had lied about the source of eggs to protect the privacy of his female researchers and that he was not aware of the Declaration of Helsinki which clearly states that his actions were in breach of ethical conduct. It also emerged that the Hwang laboratory had used egg cells in their research that had been obtained in exchange for payment.

Hwang said: 'I again sincerely apologise for having stirred concern at home and abroad', adding that because he was 'too focused on scientific development, I may not have seen all the ethical issues related to my research'.

After the press conference, which was aired on all major South Korean television networks, most of the nation's media, government ministries and public gave support to Hwang. There was an increase in the number of women who wanted to donate their eggs for Hwang's research. At one time, 15,000 women formed themselves into a 'We love HSW' fan club.

But the scandal took a dramatic turn on December 15, when Roh Sung-il announced to the press that nine of the eleven stem cell lines cited in *Science* had been faked and that tests showed those nine lines shared identical DNA, implying that they had come from the same source. Roh stated that 'Professor Hwang, admitted to fabrication' and that Hwang and another co-author had asked *Science* to withdraw the paper.

Two major press conferences were held on Korean television networks on December 16; one with Hwang followed by the other with his former colleague, Roh Sung-il. Hwang started his by claiming that the technology to make stem cells exists. He acknowledged the falsifications of research data in the paper, attributing them to unrecoverable 'artificial mistakes'. He said that there was a problem with the original lines caused by contamination, and that if he were given ten more days he could re-create the stem cell lines. He accused Dr Kim Sun-Jong, a former collaborator, of 'switching' some of the stem cell lines.

In his press conference only minutes later, Roh Sung-il rebutted Hwang's accusation, saying Hwang was blackmailing MizMedi and Kim Sun-jong. He maintained that at least nine of the eleven stem cell lines were fakes and that Hwang was simply untrustworthy. Adding fuel to the fire, MBC broadcasted the content of the cancelled *PD Su choop* show, which substantiated Roh's claim.

Seoul National University set up an emergency panel to investigate the allegations. Hwang's laboratory was sealed off and testimonies collected from him, Roh and others involved with the scandal. Its verdict, announced in late December, was that Hwang had intentionally fabricated stem cell research results, creating nine fake cell lines out of eleven, and added that the validity of two remaining cell lines was yet to be confirmed. The panel stated that Hwang's misconduct is 'a grave act damaging the foundation of science'. Hwang's claim of having used only 185 eggs to create stem cell lines was also denied by the panel, which indicated that more eggs may have been used in the research process. The panel further confirmed that there were no patient-matched embryonic stem cells in existence and that Hwang's team didn't have the scientific data to prove any of the stem cells had ever been made.

In its final report, published on January 10, 2006, the panel announced additional discoveries: that, contrary to Hwang's claim of having used 185 eggs for his team's 2005 paper, his own lab records showed that at least 273 eggs were used. The panel also discovered that Hwang's team was supplied with an astonishing 2,061 eggs between November 28, 2002, and December 8, 2005. Hwang's claim of not having known about the donation of eggs by his own female researchers was also refuted. In fact, it was discovered that Hwang himself had distributed egg donation consent forms to his researchers and personally escorted one to the MizMedi Hospital for the egg extraction procedure.

In conclusion, the investigating group declared that Hwang's 2004 *Science* paper was fabricated and that his team intentionally fabricated the data in both the 2004 and the 2005 papers, describing the fakery as 'an act of deception targeted to both the scientific community and general public'. In the face of such scientific misconduct, *Science* magazine retracted both of Hwang's papers the very next day.

There was, however, one small consolation for the disgraced Hwang. The panel confirmed that his team actually succeeded in cloning the dog they named Snuppy.

Hwang held his second major grovelling press conference on January 12, but still he did not admit to cheating. Instead, he put the blame on other members of his research project for having deceived him with false data. He alleged a conspiracy, saying his projects had been sabotaged and that material had been stolen. Hwang maintained that two of his eleven forged stem cell lines had been maliciously switched for cells from regular, not cloned, embryos.

He said that cloning human stem cells was certainly possible and that he had the technology to do it – and if he were given six more months he could prove it. That as a slight extension of the 'ten days' he'd said he needed to re-create stem cells that he asked for back on December 16, 2005.

That same day, Seoul prosecutors raided Hwang's home for files and evidence to start a 'criminal investigation'. On February 9, 2006, Seoul National University suspended Hwang as a professor, together with six other faculty members of his team. He was finally dismissed from the university on March 20.

On May 12, he was indicted on charges of fraud, embezzlement and breach of the country's bioethics law. Prosecutors also brought fraud charges against the three stem cell researchers, Yoon Hun-soo, Lee Byeong-chun and Kang Sung-keun. It was claimed that Hwang had embezzled £2.8 billion out of some £40 billion research funds for personal purposes and for the illegal purchase of ova used in his experiments.

It was the biggest fall possible for a national hero and a previously adulatory public finally learned how the man they had revered was a cheat, liar and thief.

In a bid to discover how the missing funds had been spent, investigators spent months tracking some £24.6 billion awarded for research – part of Hwang's £36.9 billion funds raised through state support and private donations. Investigators said Hwang used bank accounts held by relatives and subordinates to receive about £475 million given by private organisations. He allegedly laundered the money by withdrawing it all in cash, breaking it up into smaller amounts and re-depositing it in various bank accounts. Hwang, it was claimed, also withdrew £140 million worth of funding to buy gifts for his sponsors, including politicians and other prominent social figures. He also allegedly misappropriated a further £26 million of research funds.

In all, Hwang was suspected of embezzling for his personal use £600 million provided by private foundations, on multiple occasions from 2001 to 2005. He was also accused of illegally paying some £38 million to 25 women who provided ova for his research in the first eight months of 2005. Hwang was further accused of giving several dozen politicians about £55 million towards political funds from 2001 to 2005. He allegedly provided £14 million to executives of large companies that provided financial support for his research. The prosecution claimed Hwang wired about £200 million to a Korean American, identified only as Kang, in September 2005 and received the same amount in US currency from him when the scientist visited the United States two months later. Also in 2005, Hwang was awarded £2 billion research funds from SK Group and the National Agricultural Cooperative Federation based on his fabricated stem cell research results.

Meanwhile, investigators said Lee Byeong-chun and Kang Sung-keun, both professors of veterinary science at Seoul National University, embezzled about £300 million of donations and £100 million given from state funds by inflating research-related expenses. Yoon Hyun-soo, a biology professor at Hanyang University, also embezzled £58 million won from the research fund managed by MizMedi Hospital.

Among officialdom, Hwang's increasingly bizarre explanations for his behaviour fell on deaf ears – including one claim, made by him in a public statement in July 2006, that that he spent part of £500 million in private donations in attempts to clone extinct Russian mammoths and Korean tigers.

The South Korean government banned Hwang from research using human eggs and he was stripped of all government honours and funds, including the title 'Supreme Scientist'. But as the investigation continued and the revelations about misspent funds grew to astounding proportions, there was some slight consolation for Hwang. Although he had deceived the world about being the first to create artificially cloned human embryos, it was acknowledged that he had contributed to a major breakthrough in the field of stem cell research. The processes he pioneered may offer a method for creating stem cells that are genetically matched to a particular woman for the treatment of degenerative diseases.

In September 2007, Hwang left South Korea for Thailand 'to escape controversy and continue his research'. While still facing charges of embezzlement and faking his research, he nevertheless insisted that he would one day be proved to have created the first cloned human stem calls. And his many supporters, including patients suffering from chronic diseases, were equally insisting that their 'Supreme Scientist' had been no more than an unwittingly victim of his own genius and enthusiasm.

CHAPTER 10

'Laird' of Tomintoul

In the bar of the Gordon Hotel, they still raise an occasional glass 'to the Laird of Tomintoul'. After all, he did improve the Scottish village no end, with major renovations to the hotel itself and support for local businesses and for social activities like the Tomintoul Highland Games. There is still a sneaking regard for the aristocratic Anthony Williams, even though locals now know that he was no 'laird' at all.

Williams was a soft-spoken phoney who milked his employers of millions to fund the village's regeneration – and his own lavish lifestyle. But when the law finally caught up with him, celebrations at Scotland Yard were decidedly muted, considering that the Fraud Squad had seldom nabbed an embezzler on such a scale. Had the criminal been anyone else, they would have heartily welcomed the attention, the glory and the headlines that arose from this high-profile case. Instead, the fraud busters of London's Metropolitan Police could only bury their heads in their hands in shocked disbelief. For the villain they had nabbed was one of their own. Anthony Williams was deputy director of finance – at Scotland Yard!

During twelve years of lies, deception and downright theft, Williams had filtered away £5 million of funds that should have been spent on the Yard's undercover operations. He had used it to finance a secret life, which had him opening bank accounts around the world, living as a nobleman, 'owning' virtually an entire Scottish village and recognised as a man of considerable substance and property just about everywhere else.

There may have been some who envied or even admired one of the twentieth century's cheekiest conmen but others, like Sir Paul Condon, the Metropolitan Police Commissioner, were left to pick up the pieces of the biggest, most humiliating inside-job ever. At a press conference, Sir Paul offered the people of London an 'unreserved apology', admitting he was 'angry and embarrassed that the courageous work of police officers had been betrayed'. The unprecedented apology was the end of an incredible and intriguing trail of corruption which led to 55-year-old Williams being sentenced to seven-and-a-half years' imprisonment on May 19, 1995.

The astonishing catalogue of deceit had begun with one small theft of £200 in 1981. The cash was earmarked as payment for an officer to take his seriously ill wife on holiday but the excuse was fictitious and the £200 was pocketed by Williams. Having succeeded so easily in his first attempt at crime, the mild-mannered accountant stole again and again – and kept on stealing right under the noses of Britain's nucleus of top crime-busters. He was in a convenient position to make his thefts easy for he was overseer of the Met's staff welfare fund, from which he began to make regular 'withdrawals'.

Just once, Williams got close to being caught. A colleague noticed that one sum didn't quite add up. Williams quickly paid in a cheque to cover the discrepancy. In total, the bespectacled, respected handler of police welfare funds siphoned off £7,000, money which should have gone to the hard-up and the ill. Much of the loot was used to ease Williams' own money problems caused by the ending of his first marriage: £500-a-month maintenance payments for his two daughters and a hefty overdraft.

Over the years, Williams became proud of his deception. His bravado grew – he was an accountant who could not only cook the books but make them boil. Without really knowing where he could get his hands on unlimited money, Williams opened an account at Coutts, bankers to the Queen and to the upper-crust. Williams' creation of an 'uncle in Norway' who was set to leave him a healthy inheritance not only smoothed the way with Coutts (the bank authorised a £30,000 overdraft) but was to later prove invaluable when questions were raised about his high-living ways.

In 1986, Williams was to strike gold. As deputy finance director, Scotland Yard could find no one better to handle police affairs of a highly confidential and sensitive nature. Williams was put in charge of a 'secret fund' to fight organised crime. The fund was supposedly to pay police informers and for general undercover work but only part was allocated for this purpose. In fact, for over eight years Williams administered two companies operating an anti-terrorist surveillance aircraft based at a Surrey airfield.

Throughout the period, while he was financing the running of the plane, IRA mainland bombing was at its peak and police needed an aircraft to keep watch on suspected arms caches and 'safe houses'. So secret was the project that just a handful of people within Scotland Yard knew of the operation and Williams' involvement in it. Inquiries by any curious outsider would reveal only the existence of two firms, one apparently owned by the other, running a small, fixed-wing airplane.

Such was the determination by anti-terrorist squads to control the IRA's activities that the Cessna plane was in constant use. For instance, in 1989 it was used in a successful operation leading to the capture of two IRA activists, Damien Comb and Liam O'Dhuibhir, at an arms dump on a desolate beach on the Pembrokeshire coast of South Wales. They were caught after a seven-week stake-out, codenamed Operation Pebble. It suited Williams greatly that the plane was so heavily used. Such victories against IRA terrorists meant few worries were raised over the Cessna's costs – £250,000 in the first year alone – allowing Williams to rob the fund blind.

Whatever the Cessna operation required, Williams immediately paid. No complaints were made about his speedy requisitioning of anything from aviation fuel to paperclips. What was to come to light when Williams eventually stood trial, however, was that over eight years he requisitioned £7 million – with only around £2 million actually being spent. The Old Bailey court was told: 'The defendant was allowed unlimited private access on his own discretion to the funds of the Receiver, as the Yard's financial controller was known. It was placed in a specified account. He did not have to answer to anyone. He controlled the payments in and the payments out.'

As the money rolled in, Williams was glad that he had his 'uncle' in Norway to explain away such untold wealth. The inheritance story fended off enquiries about his grand homes and grand lifestyle. And Williams certainly knew how to splash the cash around. The money was spread across banks and building societies in Scotland, London and the Channel Islands. He even paid cash for some of the many properties he acquired, one apartment was bought directly from the secret Scotland Yard fund. In 1989 alone, he stole more than £1 million.

It was remarkable that Williams' wife Kay happily accepted the 'Norwegian uncle' story to explain the couple's elevation into a style of living most people could only dream of. It was even more remarkable that no one at Scotland Yard got wind of the millionaire lifestyle of the £42,000-a-year accountant. He brought homes in Leatherhead and Haslemere, in Surrey, and a flat in London's Westminster. He rented another flat in Mayfair which cost him £2,000 a month.

Friends he lavishly entertained still marvelled at Williams' good fortune in having a foreign relative who had left him such wealth. Yet another house in New Malden, Surrey, was purchased for £178,000 cash. A holiday villa on Spain's Costa del Sol was added to the property empire. As well as Coutts, where he was given a gold bank card, Williams opened accounts at National Westminster, Standard Chartered and Clydesdale banks and the Leeds and Bradford & Bingley Building Societies. But it was in Scotland where Williams' stolen wealth allowed him to feel as if he owned the world.

Williams had fallen in love with the Highland beauty spot where he had spent several happy holidays. Tomintoul, which takes its name from the Gaelic 'Tom an t-Sabhail' ('Hillock of the Barn') was a sleepy Grampian village of 320 people, and in 1989 he decided to buy a large chunk of it. Appearing at weekends, turned out in understated country tweeds or sometimes in a kilt, Williams first purchased a modest £6,000 cottage in The Square, on which he carried out £40,000 renovations. Then there was the £120,000 Gordon Hotel, which underwent £1.5 million restoration, the old fire station (£21,000) and the Manse in Glenlivet (£192,000). Williams even had the cheek to apply to the Moray Enterprise Board for a Business Expansion Scheme grant for one of his companies,

Tomintoul Enterprises, which in turn provided £3 million towards Williams' regeneration of the little village.

The good folk of Tomintoul hailed Williams as a saviour and indeed, to them, he was. He created dozens of jobs at his hotel, pub and restaurant, which at one time employed seven chefs, and he sponsored local events including the Tomintoul Highland Games. The villagers had even more reason to believe the Lord had provided; for Williams invested £70,000 on acquiring the title Laird before taking over Tomintoul. Not content with one feudal title, Williams bought himself another eight at a cost of £144,000.

When the Laird of Tomintoul was finally arrested, the villagers could only speak well of him. 'I know what he did was wrong but it wasn't that bad,' said George McAllister, in charge of the local museum. 'Most of these fraud types spirit the money away into foreign bank accounts or investments abroad but he didn't. He put most of it back here into our wee village. It really made Tomintoul a better place. I found Tony a very charming man, very friendly, with no put-on about him at all. It's hard to understand why a clever person like him would do what he did, but he certainly benefited the village. A lot of the properties have been beautifully restored. Just look around you.'

Iain Birnie, running the village shop, said: 'So it was money from London? Big deal. They've got enough of the stuff down there anyway. It should be coming north. Tony Williams did a damn sight more good with it up here than it would ever have done down south.'

At his wood-carving shop in the village square, Donald Corr said: 'Everyone wondered where the money was coming from. We asked ourselves why was he spending it in a wee little place in the Highlands? He wouldn't have gotten it back in 100 years.'

Williams' investment in the village gained him a different kind of dividend, however: disgrace and prison. His downfall came when banks grew suspicious about the large and endless amounts of cash he was depositing. It was believed something more sinister than downright fraud was afoot. So, as obliged to under the Drugs Trafficking Offences Act, they disclosed their worries to the police. Williams's arrest came in July 1994. Two months later he was dismissed from his job.

At his trial, Williams pleaded guilty to seventeen charges of theft from the Receiver of Scotland Yard and two charges of theft from the civilian staff's welfare fund. Williams initially denied any charges relating to the welfare fund – simply, said his barrister James Sturman, because he had forgotten all about the crime. Williams asked for 535 other charges to be taken into consideration. In all, he had stolen £5,320,737 of the £7,413,761 entrusted to him over the years.

It had been a relief to Williams when he was finally caught, said Mr Sturman. Apart from a few panic-struck lies and half-truths when first arrested, Williams had fully co-operated with the police. Around £529,000 of the stolen funds had been recovered and there were hopes of a further £200,000 to £300,000, the court heard. The lawyer added that Williams felt terrible remorse for his sins and had expressed as much to priests. 'He has lied to his wife, he has lied to his friends, he has lived a lie,' said Mr Sturman.

Referring to Williams' double life in Scotland, prosecuting counsel Brian Barker QC summed up Williams' influence on the Highland village he had changed out of all recognition. He said: 'The suburban civil servant became, when he crossed the border, a nobleman and benefactor of Tomintoul.'

Despite continuing support and some quiet admiration for the accused, Williams did not call any character witnesses. He told the court: 'I don't want to put my good friends in the box to say I was honest. Obviously, I haven't been for years.' Sentencing him to six and a half years for the thefts from his employers and one year for stealing from the welfare fund, the Recorder of London, Sir Lawrence Verney, told him: 'Such crimes are inexcusable. No one minded to follow your example must be left in any doubt as to the consequences.'

Williams, still bearing a healthy tan from his travels, left the dock to begin his sentence, clutching the carrier bag which contained what seemed now his only worldly goods. His 47-year-old wife vowed to stand by him. She did so and, a mere three years later, the couple were seen strolling hand in hand near the open prison from where he was shortly to be allowed early release, having served only half his sentence – and with only a fraction of the missing £5 million recovered.

Meanwhile, the folk of Tomintoul had been left to pick up the pieces of a property explosion which no longer had funds available to sustain it. Jobs were lost and fewer lavish shindigs graced the £25,000 carpet of the bar of the Gordon Hotel. But the village devised one final reminder of the high-living fraudster: a new brand of ale cheekily labelled 'Laird of Tomintoul Beer' and bearing a label in the shape of a Metropolitan Police helmet.

Two investigations were launched into just how Williams got away with his criminal activities for so long, one concentrating on the civil welfare fund, the other on the secret fund. They did not make happy reading for the red-faced top brass at Scotland Yard. Williams himself had a brief but succinct explanation for his crimes. In a rare interview, he told *The Times* of London: 'I discovered this bloody great bucketful of money. I went from the need to pay off a few debts to what can only be described as greed. There are no excuses.'

CHAPTER 11

'Count' who was King of the Cons

Victor Lustig – or 'Count Lustig' as he preferred to be called – liked to live in high style. This he achieved by fraud of the most ambitious kind. And such was his audacity that he may justifiably be regarded as the most audacious conman of all time.

Lustig already had a track record of trickery, having been arrested 45 times in his criminal career, before he set up his most masterly scam, in a Paris hotel in 1925. His almost unbelievable aim…to sell the city's most famous landmark, the Eiffel Tower!

Victor Lustig was born in Hestinne, Czechoslovakia, in 1890, and found himself in Paris when his father decided he should become a student at the Sorbonne. He soon discovered that studying came a poor second to the Paris high life, which he financed by his skilful gambling.

The young playboy's ability to speak several languages came in useful when he later joined transatlantic liners to fleece dollars from rich American card players. He was taken under the wing of Nicky Arnstein, an expert at 'working the boats', and soon learned how to spot an easy target. The pair remained partners throughout a series of frauds in America before Lustig returned to Paris and took a room at the fashionable Hotel Crillon, overlooking the Champs Élysées. There he met up with a new partner, 'Dapper' Dan Collins. It was time for more money-making fun.

Their golden opportunity presented itself swiftly. Lustig was perusing his morning newspaper on May 8, 1925 when his eye alighted upon a report that the Eiffel Tower was in need of major repairs. The cost would be so substantial that the French government was even considering it more economic to dismantle the famous Paris landmark.

Lustig and Collins got into a heated debate. Collins thought the idea of tearing down the Eiffel Tower disgraceful; Lustig argued that, surprisingly, many French people thought the monument hideously ugly. His argument was supported by the fact that the newspaper report made no mention of public protest over the government's plans. What both men did agree on, however, was the potential for a splendid money-spinning adventure.

Lustig got to work quickly. He forged letterheads of the Ministère des Postes et des Télégraphes, the authority responsible for the Eiffel Tower, and he found out who were the main iron and steel stockholders and scrap metal dealers in and around Paris. He drew up a list of five suitably wealthy candidates for his confidence trick, and all five received official-looking invitations from the Ministère to attend a meeting at the Hotel Crillon. There they were warmly welcomed by the 'secretary to the deputy director', the dapperly attired Dan Collins. After a few minutes, the 'deputy director' himself made his impressive appearance. It was, of course, Victor Lustig.

He began with a warning: 'I must emphasise, gentlemen, that what I am going to tell you must be treated in the greatest confidence. Indeed, I should point out that before we sent you your invitations, each one of you was very thoroughly investigated. The nature of my news is so important, such a matter of national concern, that only the most trustworthy, the most serious, the most scrupulous businessmen in Paris are being let into my Ministry's little secret.'

There was a dramatic pause as Lustig waited to see what effect his words would have on the gathering. There was an expectant hush. Then he continued: 'No doubt you have read the newspaper reports. It is unnecessary for me to tell you that the Eiffel Tower, one of the more noble features of our noble city, has fallen into a serious state of disrepair. If all the work which is urgently needed is carried out, the bill will run into hundreds of thousands of francs. It is more than any of us sitting around this table could afford — and, dare I say it, more than France could afford.'

After giving the five businessmen an authoritative history lesson on the Eiffel Tower, Lustig then came to the point of his meeting. Emphasising the crucial need for confidentiality to avoid 'political ramifications', he told his audience that the Eiffel Tower was being pulled down and that the resulting mountain of 7,000 tons of scrap iron was up for sale to the highest bidder. To give further credibility to his authority, Lustig then proceeded to summarise the 'official' government specifications of the tower. It was 984 feet high, the base measured 142 yards in each direction and the inter-laced girders were made of 12,000 sections joined together by over two and a half million rivets. The scrap dealers were spellbound.

Lustig's introductory talk was followed by an invitation to the businessmen to climb into one of the 'official cars' waiting outside the hotel, and spend the afternoon viewing the Eiffel Tower. Lustig, the bogus man from the ministry, would then await the arrival of sealed bids at the Crillon Hotel. He told Poisson and the others that, because of the delicacy of the matter, the ministry could not be seen to be involved. The bids, therefore, should be addressed to 'Monsieur Dante'.

At this early stage, however, Lustig had already identified his prime 'target'. With an eye to the greedy and the gullible, he had marked down millionaire businessman André Poisson as the ideal 'purchaser' of the Eiffel Tower. Poisson was one of the provincial nouveaux riches, anxious to make a name for himself in the Parisian business world and as such was judged by Lustig to be a man who would ask fewest questions in his quest to seal the deal.

Back in his office, Poisson himself was already calculating how to raise the finance needed to make the Eiffel Tower his very own. He even considered remortgaging his home. In his imagination, he foresaw newspaper headlines about himself: 'André Poisson, The Man Who Bought The Eiffel Tower.' Even when Poisson's wife said she found it peculiar that such confidential meetings were held in a hotel room, Poisson remained unsuspicious. Lustig had had an answer for that too; he had emphasised the fact that the ministry must be seen to have no part in such controversial dealings.

Poisson was beside himself when, a few days later, Lustig knocked on his door and told him his bid had been successful. Poisson was now required to bring a certified cheque for a quarter of his bid price to the same suite of rooms at the Crillon. Upon receipt of this, he would receive the necessary documents confirming his ownership of the Eiffel Tower and the terms on which he would be permitted to demolish it.

And so it was that Poisson arrived at the Hotel Crillon on May 20, 1925, full of the joys of spring. He had every reason to feel especially good about himself because today was the day he was going to make history. He was right, of course, but not for the reason he expected. He was about to go down in the annals of fraud as the victim of one of the most audacious hoaxes ever perpetrated.

But as he approached the suite of rooms to meet Lustig, doubts began to creep in. He remembered his wife's suspicions about the whole business. He fingered the cheque in his pocket. It represented nearly all his assets. Lustig sensed Poisson's apprehension and knew he had to act quickly. It was already after 2pm and the banks in Paris closed at 2.30pm. That cheque had to be cashed today so that he and Collins could be on their way.

Lustig embarked on some clever play-acting. He adopted a nervous tone to explain that although he was in an important and influential position, his salary was but a pittance. He had to rely on 'commissions' to earn a proper wage. Perhaps, he hesitated, Monsieur Poisson could see his way clear to offer a commission too.

'A bribe you mean?' blurted out the astonished Poisson. Lustig merely smiled politely. Poisson relaxed. He knew all about bribes. They were a necessary evil he had come across in many a business transaction before. Now he knew the man from the ministry had to be genuine. Poisson reached inside his pocket, drew out his wallet and pulled out the substantial wad of banknotes he always kept for such occasions. Lustig leaned over and, still smiling, helped himself to several thousand francs. Poisson returned his wallet to his pocket and then handed over his cheque to Lustig. The two men shook hands. It had been a very satisfactory meeting all round.

That afternoon, Lustig and Collins boarded a train to Vienna, where they lay low. Every day they avidly read the newspapers, waiting for the storm to break – but not a word about the hoax ever appeared. Poisson had obviously decided his pride was worth more than the bundle of money he had so readily handed over. The fraudsters waited patiently for two weeks for any repercussions. Then, safe in the knowledge that the police had not been informed of their con-trick, they made new plans... to sell the Eiffel Tower all over again!

And so the dodgy duo headed once again for Paris. The same deception as before was put in motion only this time, the victim, realising he had been fooled, went straight to the police. Lustig and Collins fled from Paris, the two confidence tricksters at last parting company.

Lustig went to America and continued duping easy targets. These included wealthy but greedy Herman Loller, to whom he sold a 'money-making machine'. Lustig even demonstrated how the machine could duplicate banknotes. A little careful preparation beforehand ensured the notes produced were genuine. So when Loller took them to a bank, their acceptance could not help but convince him the machine would make him even wealthier. Loller bought the machine from Lustig for $25,000. Amazingly, it was a year before Loller reported his worthless purchase to the police, having spent months believing that he had not properly mastered the machine. Lustig pulled the same stunt on a sheriff in Oklahoma. When the lawman tracked him down in Chicago to complain, Lustig 'made' some banknotes for him. Sadly for the sheriff, Lustig had used counterfeit money. The sheriff found himself on the wrong side of the law when he tried to use the cash and was jailed.

Lustig's cheating career continued. He even bravely attempted to swindle ruthless Mafia boss Al Capone. He took $50,000 off Capone, telling him he could double it on Wall Street. In fact, Lustig could think of no scheme to double the money, so he boldly returned to Capone, handed the $50,000 back and admitted he had failed. Lustig's feigned humiliation at having let such a great man down impressed Capone. He peeled off a wad of notes and gave them to Lustig as compensation.

The arch-conman went on to flood America with counterfeit money and was eventually arrested. He went on trial in December 1935 and was sentenced to fifteen years, plus another five years for an earlier escape from a federal institution. Even Lustig could not talk his way out of infamous Alcatraz prison. He served ten years before contracting pneumonia. Now an ailing man of 57, he was transferred to the Medical Centre for Federal Prisoners in Springfield, Missouri, where he died on March 9, 1947. The death certificate recorded his occupation as 'apprentice salesman' – a description that failed to do justice to 'Count' Victor Lustig's colourful, cheating life.

CHAPTER 12

Landmark Cases

Selling the Eiffel Tower is such an incredible confidence trick that one would think it was unique in the annals of con-artistry. Far from it. It takes just three ingredients to create confidence tricks of similarly monumental proportions... a famous landmark, a fool gawping at it and a fraudster to dupe him.

Enter, in the latter category, a canny Scotsman named Arthur Furguson. A small-time actor, Furguson had found meagre fame, and even less fortune, touring with repertory companies in his homeland and in the North of England; he deserved better for, as an actor, he was extremely convincing. Furguson had once played the role of an American duped by a conman, and this gave him the idea for some of the most brazen confidence tricks in history.

Within just a few weeks in 1925, Furguson conned three American tourists into 'buying' three of London's best-known landmarks: Big Ben, Nelson's Column and Buckingham Palace.

Nelson's Column was the first to go. Erected in honour of the great Admiral Horatio Nelson after his naval victory over the French, the column stands in London's Trafalgar Square. Also standing in the square and gazing up at the column on this particular day was a tourist from Iowa. Furguson approached him. 'The statue atop that column is of England's greatest naval hero, victor of the Battle of Trafalgar in 1805,' announced Furguson. 'It's such a pity that it is having to be dismantled to help repay Britain's war loan from the United States.'

The American was horrified. In the conversation that ensued, Furguson established that the man was not only a 'lover of fine architecture' but also extremely rich. In that case, suggested the Scot, he really ought to note that he, Arthur Furguson, was none other than the Ministry of Works official entrusted with the sad task of arranging the sale. There was already a long queue of potential buyers, warned the talkative trickster, but if there was a chance of the monument going to such a fine new home as Iowa, then he guaranteed his best efforts to see that his new-found friend would get this great edifice.

The man from Iowa was hooked. He pleaded with Furguson to let him jump the queue for Nelson's Column. Eventually, the Scot agreed to telephone his superiors there and then. Within minutes he was back with the good news that, for an immediate cheque in the sum of £6,000, he could have the monument and dismantle it as soon as he liked. The cheque was written and a receipt exchanged for it, accompanied by the name and address of the 'authorised' demolition company. The afternoon was now drawing on and the company had closed for the day. But the next morning the American was on the phone to them — but all he heard from the other end were gales of laughter. Tourists are always told that when in doubt, they should ask a London bobby. A bemused constable heard the American's story and led him to Scotland Yard nearby. There, at last, the penny dropped. But so did £6,000, for Furguson had already cashed the cheque and disappeared.

Arthur Furguson was now flushed with success, as well as whisky and grander plans. Within weeks, Scotland Yard again heard of his amazingly barefaced cheek when an American complained that he had bought Buckingham Palace for £2,000 yet the Royal Family would not allow him through the gates. Only days later, a third transatlantic tourist told them he had paid good money for Big Ben, the popular name for the clock tower alongside the Houses of Parliament. Furguson had accepted a knockdown price of £1,000 for it.

Police chiefs within the red-brick edifice of Scotland Yard were less than pleased that their neighbouring buildings were being hawked on the streets of London. Might not they be next? However, attempts to trap the elusive Furguson came to nought. So impressed was the conman with the generosity of the American people that he had decided to emigrate there.

Once in the United States, the Scotsman's career of con-artistry continued unchecked. 'Think big' was Furguson's motto, so he offered a Texan cattle rancher a 99-year lease on a large white building in Washington. The rent was $100,000 a year, with the first year paid in advance. The Texan handed over the cash in exchange for a worthless lease on the White House!

Having attempted to dispossess the President of the United States, Furguson then attempted to do likewise to its most famous lady. In Manhattan he encountered a gullible Australian on a visit from Sydney, to whom he spun a yarn about New York Harbour's waterways being widened. The unfortunate consequence of this modernisation programme, explained Furguson, was that the Statue of Liberty was to be dismantled and sold. If relocated to the southern hemisphere, would it not look just fine re-erected on Pinchgut Island in the middle of Sydney Harbour? The unsuspecting Australian was given a guided tour of the statue, a gift to New York from the people of France. The Australian then asked a passer-by to take a photograph of himself with the famous torch-carrying lady in the background to show the folks back home. Unfortunately for Furguson, he too was in the picture.

The Australian's next call was to his New York bank, where he made an immediate application for a loan of $100,000, the price being asked by Furguson. The bank manager was more suspicious, however, and urged his client to check with the New York Police Department. Having shown them the photograph of himself with the phoney 'city official', detectives swiftly swooped on Furguson, who ended up with a five-year jail sentence.

Upon his release in 1930, Arthur Furguson removed himself to the gentler climes of Los Angeles, where he found the pickings modest but satisfactory. He perpetrated a further string of minor confidence tricks from his luxurious new home, avoiding the interest of the Californian police until his death in 1938.

Another smooth-talker who specialised in selling landmarks to unwary tourists was George Parker, one of the most audacious conmen in American history. Operating mainly in New York at the beginning of the Twentieth Century, he set up a fake office in the city to handle his real estate swindles. He produced impressive forged documents to prove that he was the legal owner of whatever property he was selling, which, over the years, included the Statue of Liberty, the original Madison Square Garden, the Metropolitan Museum of Art and General Grant's Tomb. When touting the latter, he posed as Grant's grandson.

Parker's favourite public landmark, however, was the Brooklyn Bridge, which he sold twice a week for years. He convinced his gullible purchasers that they could make a fortune by charging tolls for access to the roadway. More than once, police had to remove naive buyers from the bridge as they tried to erect toll barriers. In America, his exploits gave rise to the phrase used to indicate that someone is gullible... 'And if you believe that, I have a bridge to sell you!'

Parker was thrice convicted of fraud and in 1928 was sentenced to a life term in Sing Sing Prison. He died in 1936, mourned by both prisoners and warders as a highly entertaining story-teller.

The golden age of such 'landmark' cases of con-artistry, as practised by the likes of Parker, Furguson and Victor Lustig, seem to have been between the two World Wars. Indeed, one would think that after Lustig's incredible Eiffel Tower hoax, no one would ever make the same mistake again. Yet a barefaced attempt by English conman Stanley Lowe to repeat a fellow confidence trickster's scam shows there is no limit to what a determined fraudster will attempt.

Just after the Second World War, Lowe managed to persuade a wealthy Texan that the Eiffel Tower had been so badly damaged by the war that the city's officials had decided to sell it off, the historic monument's scrap value being a mere

$40,000. The Texan fell for the story. Luckily for him, the attempted fraud was uncovered in time and Lowe was sentenced to nine months in jail.

The Eiffel Tower deception was just one in a series in Lowe's conning career. His speciality was disguise, and he regularly took on the persona of different characters. Wearing clerical gowns, Lowe once persuaded a Japanese tourist to contribute $100,000 to an 'appeal' to help restore London's historic St Paul's Cathedral. Another of Lowe's roles was as an Oscar-winning Hollywood producer called Mark Sheridan, seeking investors for a potential box-office success. On other occasions, he would become Group Captain Rivers Bogle Bland, a former flyer working undercover for the British government on a top-secret mission. Despite the ludicrous name he had chosen for the fictitious war hero, he still managed to convince people to part with their money.

Lowe did not always want to prise cash from people, however; sometimes he just enjoyed inventing stories. It was a pastime he had perfected early in life when his home was an orphanage in North London. Lowe drifted into crime at an early age, quickly realising that you had to think on your feet to wriggle out of tricky situations. There was the time when the owner of a Mayfair apartment caught him stealing. Calmly, he explained: 'Madam, this is an emergency. I was just passing when I saw a man attempting to hurl himself from the window.' Then he coolly walked off with his pockets full of the woman's jewellery.

It was Lowe's talent for escaping justice that enabled him to lead a champagne lifestyle. He wore hand-made shoes and shirts, stayed at the famous George V Hotel in Paris and went on exotic holidays. One of his plots was aimed at funding this lifestyle on a conveniently regular basis. Lowe smooth-talked his way into a job as a footman at Marlborough House, home of Queen Mary, where he planned to lift as much as he could lay his hands on. But his taste for high living was his downfall. One day he arrived for his footman's job wearing a designer suit and driving a brand new Jaguar car – which he had just stolen. Suspicions were naturally aroused, as Lowe's lifestyle seemed a little extravagant on a weekly wage of £6.

When questioned by officers of the law, the conman told them: 'The Queen is surrounded by priceless possessions and I had nothing. It's not that I'm disloyal to our beloved Royal Family. I just decided she should be punished for her greed.' A prison sentence followed and, when he was released, Lowe seemed to have lost his trickster's confidence. He was never the same villain again, eventually ending his days in a humble one-room apartment. The glory days for the man who fancied himself as a modern Robin Hood – 'I want to rob the rich,' he once said – were finally over.

CHAPTER 13

Catch Me if you Can

His escapades were so fantastic that a Hollywood movie was made about him. *Catch Me If You Can* was the Stephen Spielberg biopic of confidence trickster Frank Abagnale, with Leonardo DiCaprio playing the conman and Tom Hanks the FBI officer chasing him. 'The true story of a real fake,' was how the film was billed. 'Every scam he pulls in the movie is what he pulled in real life,' Spielberg vowed at the launch. 'There's an awful lot of authenticity in it,' said Hanks, with DiCaprio adding that the plot was 'more fantastic than anything Hollywood could make up'. Wherein hangs a mystery, because some critics alleged that a lot of Abagnale's life story had indeed been made up – by the conman himself. So, was *Catch Me If You Can* all truth or partly fiction? Was Abagnale a resourceful fraudster or a Walter Mitty fantasist? Or a bit of both?

In the case of Frank Abagnale, it is almost impossible to separate fact from fiction. The only certainties surround his early years. Born in 1950 and brought up in the New York suburb of Bronxville, where his family ran a stationery shop, his father became his first victim when the 15-year-old used his gas station credit card to buy tyres, batteries and anything else he could sell for a wad of dollars to impress girlfriends. The fraud was discovered only when the credit card company asked Abagnale Sr. why he had bought fourteen sets of tyres and 22 batteries in three months.

Frank was sent to a private reform school but it had little effect and, within a year, he had moved back to New York City where he learned the art of 'paperhanging': cashing cheques issued on empty bank accounts. The only problem was that bank-tellers asked too many questions of a 16-year old, so he set about creating a new identity for himself. An airline pilot, seen as a glamorous profession in the 1960s, was, he correctly judged, the perfect guise.

Not for Frank the normal years of study and training, of course. The teenager 'aged' a few years by prematurely dying his hair grey, then he rang Pan Am pretending to be a pilot whose uniform had been stolen and asked where to get a spare one at short notice. The airline directed him to the Well-Built uniform company, where he was fitted out in the blue suit of a first officer – all on Pan Am's account. Then, using logos taken from a model airplane kit, he forged a staff ID card. Abagnale was suddenly a Pan Am 'co-pilot'.

Abagnale got away with this double life for two years, jetting around the world, staying in luxury hotels and wining, dining and bedding hundreds of women along the way. He would sign into hotels used by aircrew, charging his room and all expenses to the airlines. He socialised with airline staff and dated attractive stewardesses. The hotels also cashed personal cheques for crew and Abagnale took full advantage of this.

Then the conman took to the skies. Airlines allowed each other's staff to travel free, a perk known as 'deadheading', and this often placed 'co-pilot' Abagnale in the jump seat at the back of the cockpit. On several occasions, the real crew invited him to take over the controls, putting thousands of passengers briefly in his hands. The first time this happened was on a Pan Am flight between Paris and Rome when, with the aircraft cruising at 30,000ft, the captain left the cockpit to mingle with passengers in the first-class compartment while Abagnale, the perfect image of the confident aviator, slid into his seat. Frank was just seventeen and had never flown a plane before.

Almost as audacious was the stunt he pulled when he conned Pan Am into putting him in touch with a group of school-leavers who had applied to be stewardesses – and hired eight of them, all Arizona university students, to travel around Europe with him dressed as Pan Am crew. He told them it was part of a promotional tour but he was using them to boost his credibility, allowing him to cash ever-larger phoney cheques.

Abagnale's aerial career ended with a close call when he was quizzed by a suspicious FBI man at Miami Airport and, although the conman talked his way out of trouble, he decided it was time for a career change. By the time he was 21, he had worked as a doctor, a lawyer and a sociology professor, while conning banks, airlines and hotels out of $2.5 million, the equivalent of around $36 million (or £17.5 million) today.

Abagnale once used a forged medical certificate to convince a hospital in Georgia that he was a senior paediatrician. When asked for a diagnosis, he would always quiz a trainee doctor, then nod sagely and say: 'I concur.' He got away with this for nearly a year, only stopping when he was asked to give emergency treatment to a sick baby, finally realising he was out of his depth.

Again he moved on, working as an attorney in Atlanta before using forged papers to become a professor of sociology at a university in Utah. By reading one chapter ahead of his students, he was able to add his own wisdom to a subject and claimed that he was so convincing the university considered offering him a permanent post.

The FBI finally caught up with him after he had returned to his pilot's role. After an ex-girlfriend tipped off police, he was arrested in Paris and extradited to the US. But, slippery to the last, he escaped from the aircraft at New York by removing the toilet and lowering himself through the hole onto the runway. He evaded capture yet again when two FBI agents confronted him on a street in Washington DC – by persuading them that he too was an undercover FBI man.

A month later, the conman fell for the oldest trick in the police manual. When two detectives spotted him strolling down a New York street, they called out his name and he made the mistake of looking back. He was sentenced to twelve years for his crimes but was offered parole after only four, on condition that he advised the FBI how to deal with the sort of crime he had committed himself. Shortly after his release, he met his wife Kelly, whom he described as his salvation, and with whom he had three children.

As a 53-year-old ex-jailbird, Abagnale again hit the jackpot in 2003 with the release of the $40 million Steven Spielberg screen adaptation of his book, *Catch Me If You Can*. But did the movie and the autobiography that preceded it tell the truth, the whole truth and nothing but the truth?

Critics pointed to Abagnale's appearance on the Johnny Carson *Tonight Show* in the Seventies, in which he confessed to an extraordinary bank robbery that netted him thousands of dollars. He told Carson that he had placed an 'Out of Order' sign on the First National City Bank of Boston's night deposit box at Logan International airport while standing nearby in a guard's uniform, with a portable box to collect the day's takings from airline and shop staff. But journalists who investigated his claims found that the bank didn't exist, and a spokesman for the similar sounding First National Bank of Boston told them: 'It never happened at our bank, never happened in Boston and never happened to the only bank that has a night deposit box out there.'

Another Abagnale boast was that he taught sociology students at Brigham Young University in Provo, Utah, after convincing his employers he was a professor. But sociology professor Barry Johnson, who taught at the prestigious college, said: 'It's news to me. To even be considered for a position at the university you must have ecclesiastical references. Without them, you just aren't going to get in.' Another of the major confidence tricks in Abagnale's life story had him spending a year as 'Dr Frank Williams' at Cobb County General Hospital near Atlanta, Georgia, where he claimed to have headed a staff of seven interns and 40 nurses. However, administrators said they had no record of any Dr Frank Williams.

When Abagnale was questioned about his stories, he said: 'I impersonated a doctor for a few days, I was a lawyer for a few days. People have asked me to prove it but, due to the embarrassment involved, I doubt if anyone would confirm the information.'

Whatever parts of Frank Abagnale's story are truth and whatever fiction, the arch confidence trickster has done well out of his criminal career. Although he received just £20,000 for the film rights to his book, the silver-haired smooth-talker (who was once America's most wanted conman) ended a career of fraud and reinvented himself as a millionaire businessman, advising companies on white-collar crime and retelling his tales of con-artistry on the American lecture circuit. Labelling himself 'the conman who came in from the cold', Abagnale's lectures are, in the words of actor Tom Hanks, 'one of the best one-man shows you will ever see'.

CHAPTER 14

The Pilfering Patriot

I t's quite an achievement to go from rags to riches and then back to rags again. But such was the roller-coaster career of a destitute orphan grandly named Horatio Bottomley that he achieved both his rise and fall at breathtakingly breakneck speed. Intelligent and self-confident, he sought wealth and fame, women and power – then threw it all away by over-reaching himself with his ever more fantastic frauds.

Bottomley was a swindler without rival in the early years of the Twentieth Century. During a lifetime of financial villainy, he charmed people into parting with their money and usually smooth-talked his way out of trouble afterwards. The phrase 'gift of the gab' seemed to have been coined just for him.

Bottomley was born in poverty in Bethnal Green, in London's East End, in 1860 and raised in an orphanage. His first introduction to the laws he was to flout all his life came when he got a job as a solicitor's clerk. Next came a post as shorthand writer at the Law Courts. While faithfully transcribing the devious deeds of those hauled before the bewigged judges of Victorian England, Bottomley realised where his true talents lay – and determined to embark on the pursuit of money, women, fame and political power.

His first foray was into the publishing business, the natural habitat of hundreds of rogues before and since. He persuaded a group of 'friends' to invest in the business and to agree to buy a number of properties, including a printing works in Devon, for the handsome sum of £325,000. His fellow directors were less than delighted when, having parted with the money, they discovered that the properties were all owned by Bottomley himself, including the printing works, which he had only just bought for a mere £200,000.

The trickster suddenly found himself back in a courtroom,

this time in the dock. The judge listened to the damning evidence heaped against the accused, then invited him to speak in his own defence. This was Bottomley's chance to reveal his magical talent for twisting the truth. The court was dazzled by his oratory and, after half an hour, the judge became convinced that it was Bottomley, rather than his fellow directors, who had been wronged. Clearing him of all charges, the judge even suggested that Bottomley should enter the legal profession.

This then became the modus operandum of fraudster Horatio Bottomley. Between 1895 and 1905, he made a fortune promoting more than 50 companies with a total capitalisation of £20 million. He would set up the companies and sell them at inflated prices to other companies under his control, which, having milked them of funds, then went bankrupt.

It is a style of fraud that has been tried and tested before and since, but it was a tribute to Bottomley's silver-tongued sales spiel that so many eager punters fell for it. He would start a company, declare especially high dividends and watch as the share price rocketed. He would then sell his own shares at an inflated price. In the days before strict stock market controls, this would usually go undetected. Under the pressure of his own unloading of shares, the prices would invariably plummet. At this stage, Bottomley would 'come to the rescue' of investors by offering to take over the failing firm. All he asked for was a fresh injection of funds from the poor shareholders.

During the Australian Gold Rush, Bottomley financed mining operations and made a fortune by juggling funds between his many companies, despite being served with 67 writs of bankruptcy. By 1897 he had made more than £3 million from his Australian ventures alone. The East Ender born into poverty now lived like a lord. His childhood days in an orphanage forgotten, he mixed with the highest in the land, he and his respectable wife accepted at the dinner tables of the aristocracy. Unbeknown to his hosts and his spouse, however, he kept a succession of young mistresses in love nests throughout the country.

Horatio Bottomley had money, women and fame. What he lacked was political power. This he remedied by a string of much publicised charitable ventures, by which he 'bought' his way into Parliament. Elected to represent the poverty stricken London constituency of Hackney South, Bottomley spent most of his time living the life of a country squire at his stately residence in Upper Dicker, near Eastbourne, Sussex.

In further pursuit of power and respectability, Bottomley returned to the world of publishing, through which he had first made his ill-gotten gains. He was instrumental in founding the *Financial Times*, which was to grow into one of the most authoritative journals of the twentieth century. He also started the fiercely patriotic magazine *John Bull*, which offered its readers huge competition prizes, many of which never materialised.

There were setbacks, of course, the most dramatic of which arose from the fraudster's inveterate love of gambling. Bottomley, a racehorse owner himself, knew that the only way to be sure to win a race was to own every horse in it. And that is exactly what he decided he would do. Bottomley scoured the Continent for a racecourse that would suit his purpose in a country where racing regulations were suitably lax. The Belgian seaside resort of Blankenberg fitted the bill precisely because the racecourse there wound its way through sand dunes and the horses were often hidden from the view of spectators and officials.

On the appointed day, six horses were entered for an afternoon race – and all were owned by Bottomley. As the time of the race approached, dozens of the schemer's accomplices placed bets on his behalf. Some of the bets were on the winner, some on the precise order in which the six horses would pass the finishing post. The six jockeys, also in the pay of Bottomley, were under strict instructions as to how to perform during every yard of the course. Then disaster befell. Just before the start, a thick sea mist blew in and obscured the entire course. The jockeys could not even see the other horses, and their shouts to one another were swallowed up in the mist. All six horses galloped to the finishing post in entirely the wrong order, losing the frantic fraudster a small fortune.

Further disaster beset Bottomley in 1912 when he was forced to resign from Parliament after a particularly scandalous bankruptcy. The suspicion was also voiced that some of the amazingly generous prizes he was offering in the pages of *John Bull* were going straight into his own pocket. The outbreak of World War One rescued him from political oblivion. No journal was more jingoistic than *John Bull* in supporting the war effort.

In his tirades published in the populist organ, Bottomley urged that Germany 'must be wiped off the map of Europe', with her colonies and Navy divided between Britain and France. He campaigned for the persecution of 'Germhuns', including the internment of those living in Britain on the grounds that: 'You cannot naturalise an unnatural beast, a human abortion, a hellish fiend. But you can exterminate it.' He also attacked Labour Party members who had opposed the war, and arguing that party leaders Keir Hardie and Ramsay MacDonald should be court-martialled for high treason. MacDonald responded by claiming Bottomley to be of 'doubtful parentage, who had lived all his life on the threshold of jail'. Bottomley retaliated by producing a facsimile of MacDonald's birth certificate which showed he was illegitimate.

Bottomley toured the country using his gift of the gab to boost recruiting – always charging a healthy fee for his services, of course – and at the cessation of hostilities in 1918, he was easily re-elected as Member of Parliament for his old constituency of Hackney South with a remarkable 80 per cent of the vote. Flushed with pride and growing ambition, the crafty crook embarked on a string of fresh, fraudulent ventures. His past, however, was about to catch up with him.

During the war, Bottomley had instigated his biggest scam ever. The government had launched war-loan stock under the title Victory Bonds. Each bond, with a redemption value of £5, cost £4 and 15 shillings – a high sum at the time for the working man and woman. To 'help' them, Bottomley launched a Victory Bond Club into which the poor could pay as little as they could afford, their pennies then being invested in the £5 bonds. Bottomley was hailed as the 'friend of the little man' as an estimated half a million pounds flowed into the Victory Bond Club. In reality, however, the crook was siphoning off about £150,000 of the paupers' cash. He used £10,000 to pay off debts, he invested £15,000 on a risky business venture of his own, and he squandered another £15,000 gambling on the horses.

When one of his former partners, Reuben Bigland, accused him of fraud, Bottomley foolishly sued for criminal libel, before back-tracking and dropping the case. But the alarm was raised and in 1922 he faced an Old Bailey jury on a charge of fraudulent conversion of Victory Bond Club funds. This time the gift of the gab failed to sway the jurors, who took just thirty minutes to find him guilty on all counts.

So sure was he of public support that the master conman boasted that 50,000 ex-Servicemen would march on Westminster to stop him being jailed. They didn't and he was. The judge sentenced him to seven years' penal servitude. In Wormwood Scrubs jail, the prison chaplain once found him making mail sacks and remarked: 'Bottomley! Sewing?' To which the crook replied: 'No, reaping!'

Released on licence in 1926, the flamboyant crook vainly attempted to restore himself to public esteem. But his fortune and his credit had long evaporated. From being one of the most respected men in Britain, he was now the most despised. He started a new career as a concert-hall comedian, parading around seedy music halls with a mawkish one-man show. But in May 1933, after suffering a heart attack, he died, a broke and broken shadow of his former rabble-rousing, venomous self.

CHAPTER 15

Racing 'Certainties'

As we saw in the previous chapter, crafty gamblers like to bet on a 'sure thing' by making absolutely certain that chance plays no part in their winning or losing – or being found out. Politician and fraudster Horatio Bottomley believed that the only way to be certain to win a race was to own every horse in it. He did and he still failed to beat the unforeseen laws of chance.

Others were even more inventive, and won or lost, fraudulently or legitimately. Marginally in the latter category is the amazing coup by racing legend Barney Curley who, in 1975, made the present-day equivalent of £5 million in Ireland's biggest ever betting coup. Curley had everyone he knew place bets on a long-odds horse, Yellow Sam, which he rated highly. Then, shortly before the 'off', an associate occupied the only phone at Bellewstown racecourse, talking for 25 minutes to a non-existent hospital about a fictitious dying aunt. This prevented bookmakers hedging off-course money back to the course and calling in the shorter odds. The 20/1 odds pocketed a haul of more than £300,000.

A year earlier, another equally ingenious racing scam had been rumbled, costing the perpetrators some hefty fines – and the £2.5 million in today's money that they would have pocketed had they succeeded. This is how it was to have worked...

A Scottish trainer entered a horse called Gay Future in an August Bank Holiday meeting at Cartmel. He also entered two other horses in races at other courses. A vast number of small bets were laid, backing Gay Future for a double with either of the other two horses. However, at the last minute, both the other horses were pulled out of their races – the double now became a single, with a lot of money riding solely on Gay Future. At Cartmel, soap flakes were rubbed into Gay

Future's legs to give the impression the horse was sweating and to keep on-track punters from backing it, holding its odds of 10-1. The horse duly romped home in first place. Sadly for the trainer and his associate, an Irish businessman, the investigation that followed the coup resulted in hefty fines for both of them.

A similar scam was played out in the more down-to-earth world of British dog-racing in 1978. A gang entered dogs in a two-part contest: sprinting heats followed by a long-distance final. They disguised sprinters as long-distance dogs to lengthen the odds, and then placed accumulating bets before withdrawing the dogs from the second round. The whole wager then transferred to the first leg. They were rumbled and lost £400,000 of their ill-gotten winnings.

Some betting plots are as complicated as they are devious; others are almost artistic in their simplicity. One such was the infamous Trodmore Hunt horse racing scandal, the beauty of which was that the conspirators did not need to fix the race – because they didn't even bother to run one.

The Trodmore conspiracy was dreamed up in 1898, a period when there were few firm guidelines on the way horse races were run in Britain. Scores of small race meetings were held around the country, often organised by the local hunt to raise money. They might be held at irregular intervals. If the crowds were large they might be repeated the following year; if poorly attended, which was more usually the case, they might not. A clerk of the course would write to one or all of the racing publications asking them to print race cards and results.

Bank holidays being a favourite date to stage minor meetings, the sporting press usually found itself inundated with requests at this time. The newspapers resigned themselves to printing as many cards as possible in the hope of keeping everybody happy. Monday August 1, 1898, was a bank holiday and, when a few weeks before, a letter arrived at the offices of *The Sportsman* from the 'Trodmore Race Club', no suspicions were aroused. The letter politely requested that the journal devote space in its pages to announce the club's first full meeting and to add the Trodmore card to the list of those printed in advance of the holiday. According to the letter, the first race would start at 1.30pm and the last at 4pm. The request was neatly written on high quality notepaper with a lavish, printed letterhead in the name of the Trodmore Race Club of Cornwall, and was signed by 'G. Martin, Clerk of the Course'.

The editor inserted the race card without a second thought but did not, at that stage, concern himself with getting hold of the results of the days racing. Before that became a problem, however, a second letter arrived at *The Sportsman*. It was from a reader who said that, having noticed the Trodmore Hunt card in the editor's illustrious journal, he planned to attend the meeting in Cornwall. He would be happy to wire the starting prices and full results to the newspaper if he was paid a small consideration for his time and trouble. The editor agreed.

The trap had been set and the sporting journalists had fallen headlong into it. For there was, of course, no such person as Mr Martin, no helpful reader – indeed no horses, no jockeys, and no race planned whatsoever. There were, however, an awful lot of bets to be placed. And but for a bizarre quirk of fate, the bookies would have been seriously stung, a gang of fraudsters would have got seriously rich and no one else would have been any the wiser.

The crooked syndicate who had dreamed up the Trodmore Hunt found the latter part of their plan – the actual placing of sufficient wagers – to be the most difficult. A huge amount of money had to be wagered on the fictitious race to make the operation worthwhile, yet it would have to be distributed in small sums to avoid suspicion. The larger bookmakers, who generally dealt on credit, could not be used because they took time to pay out the winnings. So the phoney punters had to rely on small-time street bookmakers who, out of commercial necessity, were a naturally suspicious breed.

It was judged foolhardy to slap large wagers on horses running in a meeting no one had ever heard of. So a large-scale map of London was pinned to the wall and divided into segments. Each punter was assigned a sector in which he would seek out every street bookie and place with him a small bet on the Trodmore race. In a further attempt to avoid suspicion, the dodgy punters were ordered to adhere to the following strict code of conduct. 1. Approach each bookmaker once only, so that no one bookie would get two punters wanting to bet on the same minor race. 2. Bet not only on the Trodmore card but on one other race meeting as well. 3. If any bookmaker raises questions about the Trodmore meeting, show him the relevant page of *The Sportsman*. 4. If he remains suspicious, the golden rule is to smile sweetly and walk away.

It would only have taken one bookmaker with a reasonable knowledge of the geography of the West Country to have discovered that there was no such place as Trodmore. As it happened, no bookie consulted his map of the British Isles and by 1pm on Bank Holiday Monday, August 1, every penny of stake money – several hundred pounds, at the very least – had been wagered. The following day, the results of the five races were duly published in *The Sportsman*, along with the starting prices. The winners were: Reaper (5-1 nap), Rosy (also 5-1), Spur (2-1), Fairy Bells (7-4), Curfew (6-4) and Jim (5-4). It was a most undramatic list, none of the odds being sufficiently long-priced to make the bookies uncomfortable. Even so, the largest stakes had been on the 5-1 nags.

This was the point at which fate took a hand in this extraordinary charade. Journalists at *Sporting Life*, the rival paper to *The Sportsman*, had spotted the Trodmore results in the other paper and had swiftly copied them for their own issue the following day. The syndicate had deliberately not contacted *Sporting Life* for fear that doubling the number of people involved would have also doubled the opportunities for errors.

Their caution was well justified. For in their haste to reproduce the Trodmore results for Wednesday's paper, a printer at the *Life* wrongly punched out the starting price of Reaper as 5–2 instead of 5–1. Whereas most bookies had paid out on Tuesday on the basis of the results in that morning's *Sportsman*, a few who had been hit hardest delayed for as long as possible. When Wednesday dawned, they naturally checked the odds in the rival *Sporting Life* and found them different – which made the slow paying bookies feel edgy and the early payers distinctly angry.

Only then was the most obvious check made: as to where in Cornwall lay the racecourse of Trodmore. Map-makers, Post Office officials and bemused Cornishmen were all consulted to no avail. Trodmore did not exist. The police were called in and the finger of suspicion was pointed at the editor of *The Sportsman*, his printers and even the sub-editor who had been ordered to insert the card. There was no proof against any of them, although the consensus of opinion was that the plot had been hatched by a group of Fleet Street journalists. By this time, however, the crafty conmen who had formed the Trodmore syndicate had smartly vanished – along with all the profits from the 'Race That Never Was'.

CHAPTER 16

Evangelists who fell from Grace

A s the Lord giveth, so he taketh away.' In the case of television hot gospeller Jim Bakker, the Lord gaveth him too much and eventually had to taketh it ALL away. Bakker was head of an organisation called PTL. It stood for Praise The Lord but it also spelt money. Throughout the 1980s boom in 'televangelism' in America, Bakker reached the very top of his vocation through a tear-stained style of Bible-punching which had the viewers sending in untold millions of dollars. Peak viewing – and therefore peak earning time – was the *Jim And Tammy Bakker Show*, an extraordinary double-act of syrupy sweetness and light with his blonde, bronzed, mascara-daubed wife.

Born James Orson Bakker in Musegon, Michigan, on January 2, 1940, Bakker had met his future bride, then Tammy Faye LaValley, in 1960 while they were Bible students at North Central University in Minneapolis. Bakker had attended the university after what he described as a 'turnaround' from his wild youth. It was also in 1960 that Bakker attended a revival meeting conducted by a minister called Oral Roberts and realised the potential of selling religion through showbusiness. The Bakkers married on April 1, 1961, and went on to have two children, Tammy Sue (Sissy) Bakker Chapman in March 1970 and Jamie Charles (Jay) Bakker in December 1975.

Jim Bakker was ordained in 1964 and that same year set off with his wife on the path to evangelical excellence when they started work at the Christian Broadcasting Network, which at the time had an audience of only several thousand. The chairman and founder of the organisation, the first Christian network in America, was Pat Robertson, who went on to become one of the country's most influential religious broadcasters. The Bakkers helped boost the CBN's viewing figures by getting Robertson to change his signature *700 Club* show from a nightly telethon to a talk and variety progamme. It went on to become one of the longest-running and most successful televangelism programmes.

The couple also developed a daily children's show called *Come on Over* which was an immediate success. The close relationship with Robertson was good for Jim Bakker's career but it also provoked jealousy amongst others who worked at CBN. When, in 1972, the Bakkers decided to leave and go their own way, some members of staff trashed the sets used by the couple – and even destroyed the puppets used in their children's shows.

Arriving in California, the couple formed Trinity Broadcasting with Paul Crouch, who was later to make it the biggest Christian network in the world. It was here the Bakkers created their daily talk show *Praise the Lord*. Their relationship with Crouch was short-lived and the parties separated with the agreement that Crouch kept Trinity Broadcasting and the Bakkers kept the PTL initials – although they waivered between PTL standing for *Praise the Lord* and an altered version, *People That Love*.

The Bakkers relocated to Charlotte, North Carolina, and began their own show, *The PTL Club*, on January 13, 1974. It was in the same *Tonight Show* format that Bakker had convinced Pat Robertson to adopt. The show was a huge success, picked up by nearly 100 stations, with an average viewing figure of more than twelve million. At the height of their ministry, the Bakkers were watched by almost fourteen million people across America. Before long, the Bakkers had established their own network The PTL Television Network (also known as PTL – The Inspirational Network).

What he lacked in stature, Jim Bakker made up for in evangelical charisma. And among the more appealing characteristics of the couple's enthusiastic approach to their faith was their readiness to accept anyone regardless of colour, creed, sexual orientation or a criminal past. They preached, they appealed and, of course, the money rolled in.

By the early 1980s, Jim and Tammy Bakker had built a theme park, with shopping mall and hotel, at Fort Mills, South Carolina. Officially described as a 'Christian-themed retreat and gospel park', others dubbed it 'Christian Disneyland'. Titled Heritage USA, the 2,300-acre park attracted six million visitors a year and was then the third most successful park in America, at one point grossing $130 million a year. They also had a satellite system which distributed their network 24 hours a day across 1,200 channels.

Contributions from the Bakkers' devoted followers were estimated to be more than $1million a week, which went towards expanding the theme park and supporting the work of PTL. If anyone criticised their televangelical bandwagon, Bakker would respond: 'I believe that if Jesus were alive today he would be on TV.'

In fact, if Jesus were alive, he certainly would not have approved of the money-orientated, big business-minded, hypocrite that was Jim Bakker. For the minister hid a secret from his generous flock. He had taken a church secretary, Jessica Hahn, to a hotel in Clearwater Beach, Florida, in 1980. Bakker allegedly drugged and had sex with Jessica, then said a short prayer before returning to the pulpit to admonish his flock for not following God's ways. It was a particularly unsavoury one-night stand. But it was to lay dormant for seven years until it was revealed on March 19, 1987. At the same time, Tammy Bakker's on-off dependency on drugs also came to light.

When the scandals broke, Jim Bakker denied allegations of rape but did admit to meeting the woman in the hotel room. However, he claimed that he was the victim of a 'diabolical plot' to oust him from his seat of power and alleged that he had been 'wickedly manipulated' in order to benefit 'treacherous former friends'. This was a thinly veiled hint that his television rival Jimmy Swaggart was jealous of his supreme position as America's Number One TV evangelist. Indeed, Swaggart had recently unleashed fire and brimstone against him over the Jessica Hahn incident and had called him a 'cancer in the body of Christ' on the *Larry King Show*.

Jim Bakker resigned in order to fight these irreligious slurs, leaving colleague Jerry Falwell to run PTL as a caretaker until he and Tammy were able to return to take their rightful place. Falwell was made of sterner stuff, however. He thoroughly dug into PTL's dealings and discovered a black hole of funds being sucked into the Bakkers' personal accounts. It was also revealed that the Bakkers, who travelled in 'his and hers' Rolls Royces and owned a 10,226 square-foot Florida condominium, complete with $60,000 gold fixtures, which the preacher had described as a 'parsonage'. There was also the question of approximately a quarter of a million dollars paid into an account to which Miss Hahn had access; it sounded very much like hush money.

While Jim and Tammy Bakker were off the air, supposedly marshalling their defence against these scurrilous allegations, they appealed to Jerry Falwell for a subsistence allowance. Falwell was astonished at their 'shopping list' of demands: $300,000 a year for him, $100,000 for her, a lakeside home in South Carolina, fees for attorneys, and wages for security guards and a maid, plus perks.

'I don't see any repentance there,' said Falwell. 'I see greed, the self-centredness, the avarice that brought them down.' He publicly decried Bakker as a liar, embezzler, sexual deviant and 'the greatest scab and cancer on the face of Christianity in 2,000 years of church history'. Donations to the PTL plummeted but, incredibly, Falwell raised $20 million to help keep the Heritage USA theme park solvent.

While Falwell was examining the PTL accounts, *The Charlotte Examiner* newspaper also scrutinised PTL's fund-raising activities between 1984 and 1987. In that period, Bakker and his PTL associates had sold 'lifetime memberships' for $1,000 or more that entitled buyers to a three-night stay each year at a luxury hotel at Heritage USA. At Bakker's trial, the prosecution alleged that tens of thousands of memberships had been sold but only one 500-room hotel was ever completed. Bakker sold more 'exclusive' partnerships than could be accommodated, while raising more than twice the money needed to build the actual hotel. A good deal of the money went into Heritage USA's operating expenses but Bakker kept $3.4 million in bonuses for himself – along with a $279,000 pay-off for Jessica Hahn's silence. Bakker, who seemingly made all the financial decisions for the PTL organisation, kept two sets of books to conceal the accounting irregularities. After carrying out their own investigation, reporters from *The Charlotte Observer* wrote a series of articles about PTL's dishonest financial activities.

Bakker and his attorney, the Reverend Richard Dortch, were defrocked from the PTL church in May 1987. The ensuing scandal went into overdrive, as the participants went their different ways. Hahn posed nude for *Playboy* magazine before becoming a saucy chat-line DJ, while Bakker became the subject of a government inquiry into his fund-raising gimmicks. It was estimated that over a three-year period the Bakkers had between them pocketed an amazing $4.8 million from PTL. The Internal Revenue Service, angry that so many tax-free donations had been misdirected, revoked PTL's charitable status. Inevitably, Bakker was indicted for fraud, along with his lawyer. In all, after a sixteen-month Federal grand jury probe, Bakker faced eight counts of mail fraud, fifteen counts of wire fraud and one count of conspiracy.

Retribution on the phoney men of God was slow coming. But in August 1989 Dortch, having agreed to testify at the ensuing Bakker trial, was jailed for eight years. Bakker, meanwhile, was still to be seen in public, making tearful appearances before the television cameras as he was wheeled back and forth for psychiatric tests. The Bakker trial itself suffered further delay when the preacher was found cowering like a whipped cur on the floor of his lawyer's office.

By way of defence, the lawyer, Harold Bender, assured the court that his client was 'a man of love, compassion and character who cares for his fellow man'. The judge, Robert Potter, was unimpressed. After a five-week trial in Charlotte, Bakker was found guilty on all counts. He was sentenced to a $500,000 fine and 45 years in jail. For once at least, the tears that flowed down Bakker's cheeks were perhaps warranted.

In early 1991, a federal appeals court upheld Bakker's conviction on the fraud and conspiracy chages but voided his 45-year sentence, together with the $500,000 fine, and ordered that a new sentencing hearing be held. At that, Bakker was sentenced to eighteen years in prison. After serving almost five years, he was granted parole in 1995 after his son, Jay, headed a letter-writing campaign to the parole board urging leniency for his father.

Jim and Tammy Bakker divorced in 1992. She went on to marry his best friend, Roe Messner, and died in 2007. Bakker married again in 1998 and has remained with his wife, Lori. A report in *The Charlotte Observer* stated that America's Internal Revenue Service still holds Bakker and Roe Messner liable for personal income taxes owed from the 1980s when they were building the PTL empire – taxes assessed after the IRS revoked the PTL ministry's non-profit status.

Bakker renounced his teachings on 'prosperity theology', saying they were misguided. In his 1996 book, *I Was Wrong*, he admitted that the first time he had read the Bible all the way through had been in prison and that it made him realise he had taken certain passages out of context. He wrote: 'The more I studied the Bible, however, I had to admit that the prosperity message did not line up with the tenor of Scripture. My heart was crushed to think that I led so many people astray. I was appalled that I could have been so wrong and I was deeply grateful that God had not struck me dead as a false prophet!' Bakker released two more books, *Prosperity and the Coming Apocalypse* and *The Refuge: The Joy of Christian Community in a Torn-Apart World*.

Bakker's son Jay, a minister at Revolution Church in New York City, wrote a book too, *Son of a Preacher Man*. In it, he said: 'The world at large has focused on my parents' preaching of prosperity, but I heard a different message – one of forgiveness and the abundance of God's love. I remember my Dad always seating a mentally handicapped man in the front row and hugging him. And when vandals burned an African American church down, Dad made sure its parishioners got the funds to rebuild. His goal was to make PTL a place where anyone with a need could walk in off the streets and have that need met.'

In January 2003, Bakker began broadcasting a daily *Jim Bakker Show* at Studio City Café in Branson, Missouri, with his wife. In January 2008, Bakker's ministry moved into a new, elaborate television studio near Branson, housed within a 600-acre development resembling Heritage USA. Most of the property is owned by associates of Bakker for, according to newspaper reports, he is still in debt to the IRS for about $6 million.

And what of the rival preacher whom Bakker had first blamed for his downfall? Fellow television evangelist Jimmy Swaggart's demise was equally scandalous...

Swaggart was a braggart, boasting that, unlike Bakker, he was incorruptible. Most of his flock believed him – until they heard what he got up to in a seedy New Orleans motel room. The evidence was in the form of photographs – handed to officials from his Assemblies of God church – of Swaggart taking a prostitute, Debra Murphee, into the hotel.

Swaggart's downfall was sweet revenge for yet another TV rival evangelist, Martin Gorman, who had also been defrocked after Swaggart accused him of 'immoral dalliances' in 1986. Gorman, who ran a successful TV show from New Orleans had launched an unsuccessful $90 million lawsuit against Swaggart for spreading false rumours. In revenge, he had hired a private detective to follow his persecutor. He discovered that Debra Murphee was regularly employed by Swaggart to perform obscene sex acts while he watched from the comfort of an armchair. Murphee went along with the lucrative sex games until the preacher suggested that she invite her nine-year-old daughter to watch also. The mother, who had a record for prostitution offences in two states, announced that she was so disgusted that she felt obliged to go public with her story. She recreated Swaggart's favourite poses for *Penthouse* magazine, and the sixteen pages of explicit pictures were deemed so hot that they had to be sealed in each issue. Murphee also went on a national media tour to publicise her revelations.

Swaggart resigned from his ministry in 1988. With his long-suffering wife Frances at his side, he sobbed in front of a congregation of 7,000 in Baton Rouge, Louisiana, and confessed to 'moral failure', adding: 'I do not plan in any way to whitewash my sin or call it a mistake.' Turning to Frances, he said: 'I have sinned against you and I beg your forgiveness.'

It could have been the end for Swaggart, who had got religion early from his Pentecostal evangelist parents, Sun and Minnie Belle. He had preached on street corners and led congregations when he was only nine. He married when he was just seventeen. Swaggart became a full-time travelling preacher in 1958 and attracted a substantial revival-meeting following throughout America's South. In 1960, he began recording gospel music albums while building up another audience via Christian-themed radio stations. By 1969, his radio programme *The Camp Meeting Hour* was being aired over numerous stations. During the 1970s, Swaggart was ordained by, and established a ministry under, the Assemblies of God. It was at this time that he decided to use television as his primary teaching medium.

By 1980, he had become the most popular television preacher in America. Around 200 TV stations broadcast his programme *The Jimmy Swaggart Telecast* and it was watched in two million homes. The Jimmy Swaggart Ministries, based in Baton Rouge, grew to include a local congregation at the Family Worship Center of more than 4,000 members, a printing and mailing production plant, a television production facility, a recording studio and a Jimmy Swaggart Bible College.

On the face of it, the preacher had not put a foot wrong in life until he fell for the charms of Debra Murphee. Because of such perfectly understandable 'moral sins', Swaggart's local church, the compassionate Louisiana Assemblies of God, was inclined to deal with him leniently and recommended a minimal three-month suspension from preaching. The national church was hardly much tougher and ordered him banished from the pulpit for a full year. Swaggart, however, unwisely defied the ban after only a few months, on the grounds that his absence would destroy his $140 million-a-year worldwide ministries. He was immediately defrocked by the Assemblies Of God.

Murphee faded from the scene after a proposed movie deal about her meetings with the dirty preacher failed to come to fruition. Swaggart, meanwhile, saw his television empire dwindle from tens of millions of viewers to mere thousands. The self-appointed mouthpiece of the Lord was merciful towards himself, telling his congregation that God had forgiven him for his sins, adding piously: 'What's past is past.'

In 1991, Swaggart was stopped for driving his car erratically – and was discovered to be sharing it with a prostitute and a pile of porn magazines.

CHAPTER 17

Spree of the Phoney 'Lady'

She was a dreamer, always believing she was destined for greater things and forever boasting about the money she would one day inherit. As plain Rosemary Aberdour, such grandiose visions must have seemed remote to neighbours in the little English village where she lived with her parents. But not even Rosemary herself could have envisaged the wealth and lifestyle to which she would soon tap into.

The plump only child of a comfortably-off middle-class family, Rosemary decided at an early age that she was good at handling other peoples' money. While living at home with her parents, a doctor and medical secretary in the village of Wickham Bishops, Essex, she had helped raise funds for her local parish church. But already she was dreaming and scheming of unlimited funds of her very own. Even she could not have imagined how much, or indeed just how it was going to come her way, but the opportunity arose when she arrived in London and found that there was as much money at her disposal as she could lay her stubby little fingers on.

That she got away with it is incredible. Yet an inner confidence, plus a winning smile, were to see her through three years of lies, fraud and fantasy as she lived the life of an aristocrat, becoming rich through the generosity of others. In one period of just three months, she went through nearly £1.5 million. There were lavish parties, expensive cars, made-to-order jewellery, luxury homes, vintage champagne and all the other trappings of a millionaire lifestyle – as led by her, under the assumed title of 'Lady Rosemary Aberdour'.

The key to Rosemary's success as a fraudster was simple: she took a course in book-keeping, a skill which was to come in exceptionally useful when she was in a position to make the books balance greatly in her favour. That opportunity came in

November 1986 when she successfully applied for a £20,000-a-year book-keeping job at London's National Hospital in Queen's Square. The hospital had a development fund, a charity launched to raise £10 million to build a new wing, and Rosemary knew she was just the person to use any donations wisely – on herself. After organising a charity ball at London's Guildhall, attended by the Princess of Wales, she realised that this was the glittering life she wanted to lead and earnestly set about achieving it.

In July 1987 Rosemary's months of devotion to duty paid off. She was promoted to the charity's deputy director. It was a position of great trust. Rosemary was to bank all the cheques that came into the National Hospital Fund and look after the accounts. At first, she stole a mere £500 to take herself on holiday but, once she realised she had got away with the theft, there was no stopping her. It was easy. Hundreds of thousands of pounds passed through her hands and she simply took the cheques for herself and fiddled the books.

Her golden opportunity came when Rosemary was asked to become chairman of the Queen's Square Ball, a separate fund-raising committee. The contents of its bank account were perused only when the date of the annual ball came around; the rest of the year, it came under no scrutiny. Rosemary had all the time in the world to deposit money stolen from the National Hospital Development Fund into the Queen's Square Ball account and to use the account as her very own nest egg. She regularly stole cheques received in the post, amounting to anything between £20,000 and £100,000 at one time. Not content with having one source of illicit income, Rosemary started forging the signature of the charity's director, Richard Stevens. She now had fraudulent cheques to increase her spending power. At last, money was no object.

When Rosemary wanted a new car, she bought one: a £70,000 Bentley. And, as always, she had an answer when asked about her purchase, made on the Queen's Square Ball account, telling top-notch car dealers H.R. Owen that the millionaire's motor model was to be a raffle prize at the ball. Then there was the £171,000 of charity cash which Rosemary spent at top jewellers Boodle & Dunthorne, and the luxury

Duped by a master conman…
Sarah Smith was one of several
victims who had their lives
ruined after falling under the
manipulative spell of Robert
Hendy-Freegard. Masquerading
as a 'secret agent', he defrauded
Sarah and her family of £300,000.

Power-mad fake 'spy'…
Robert Hendy-Freegard
turned the lives of his victims
into a humiliating charade of
fear, exploitation and
degradation. His motto: 'Lies
have to be big to be
convincing.'

Star-struck… Society con-artist David Hampton was a celebrity imposter who milked his fabricated alter-ego for all it was worth.

Secretary's stash… Despite her modest office role, Joyti De-Laurey was a major fraudster, stealing £4million from her rich employers. Her motto: 'I've got an illness only diamonds can cure.'

Bungling sex surgeon… Dr John Romulus Brinkley made a fraudulent mint out of his unique 'medical marvel' – pretending that goats' testicles would enhance men's sexual powers.

Drowning in debt…
Politician John
Stonehouse tried to
escape his creditors
and the law by faking
his own death, then
fleeing across the
world.

The loyal lover… High-flying John Stonehouse not only swapped identities, he also swapped his wife for his sultry secretary, Sheila Buckley, pictured after his release from prison.

Con-man to 'The King'... Self-styled 'Colonel' Tom Parker was the cigar-chomping manager who catapulted Elvis Presley to mega-stardom – but fleeced him mercilessly throughout his life.

Superstar who got stung... A youthful Elvis Presley pictured flanked by his manipulative manager 'Colonel' Tom Parker and US TV show host Ed Sullivan.

Master of his craft…
Ex-schoolteacher John
Myatt reproduced great
art works which were
then passed off as
originals.

Art of deception…
John Myatt helped
perpetrate what
was described as
'the biggest art
fraud of the 20th
century'.

King of clones… South Korean scientist Professor Hwang Woo-suk, pictured with one of his experimental subjects, was feted worldwide as a pioneering genius who had the potential to create carbon-copy human embryos and cure life-threatening diseases.

Clone 'genius' confesses… Unmasked for faking some of the research behind his 'miracle' breakthroughs, Professor Hwang Woo-suk faced public humiliation and the end of an illustrious career.

The 'Scottish laird'… Known as 'the Laird of Tomintoul', Anthony Williams virtually owned a Scottish village – but the money to buy it was milked from his employers, the Metropolitan Police!

King of the Cons… Victor Lustig was possibly the most audacious confidence trickster of all time – his greatest coup being to sell the Eiffel Tower not once but twice.

Under arrest… After a long career of crime, Victor Lustig – or 'Count Lustig' as he preferred to be called – was arrested and interrogated by US Treasury agents who found him in possession of vast quantities of forged dollars.

Handcuffed but still smiling… Victor Lustig, also known as the 'Bouncing Czech', spent the last years of his life in Alcatraz prison.

Lowest of the Lowe… Stanley Lowe emulated Lustig's success in selling off the Eiffel Tower. Here, Lowe is pictured at an official function in one of his many phoney guises – along with another fraudster, publisher Robert Maxwell, who was also known as a 'Bouncing Czech'.

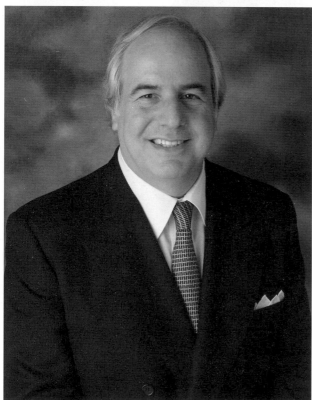

Catch Me If You Can…
Arch conman Frank
Abagnale was the unseen
star of the movie *Catch
Me If You Can*, with his
role played by Leonardo
DiCaprio. His most
renowned exploits
involved him pretending
to be an airline pilot –
which is why he dressed
for the part (above) when
he appeared as a celebrity
guest on an American
game show.

Pilfering patriot…
Horatio Bottomley
seen here, achieved
wealth and fame,
women and
political power –
then utter infamy
when his frauds
were uncovered.

Fall from grace… Jimmy Swaggart was a
braggart, boasting that, unlike some of his
fellow TV Evangelists, he was incorruptible.
The truth was more tawdry.

Hot gospeller… Jim Bakker urged his huge TV congregations to righteousness – despite secretly enjoying hot money and hot sex, while cheating on his wife Tammy (pictured with him left).

She's no lady… Self-styled 'Lady' Rosemary Aberdour blew millions of pounds of charity funds on expensive homes, lavish parties, luxury cars and designer jewellery.

Work of fiction…
Clifford Irving sold the
publishing coup of the
century, the 'authorised
biography' of billionaire
Howard Hughes – even
though he'd never even
met the man.

Unpleasant peasant… Former washerwoman Thérèse Humbert, (left in this family picture)
put her peasant past behind her and funded a lavish Paris lifestyle on the promise of a non-
existent inheritance.

Sincerely rich… Bernie Cornfeld urged on his 10,000-strong sales force with the rhetorical question: 'Do you sincerely want to be rich?' Handling £1billion of investor's money made him extremely rich but ruined others.

'A likeable bastard'… That's how a pal described Australian charmer Peter Foster, who could lay claim to the dubious title of 'World's Greatest Living Conman' because of his lifetime of scams.

Pampered pair… Former British Prime Minister's wife Cherie Blair strides out with her 'style guru' Carole Caplin. Ever the charmer, Peter Foster became Mrs Blair's bent financial adviser – by first becoming Miss Caplin's lover.

Pacific pursuit… Peter Foster's criminal career, from peddling 'miracle' slimming pills to pampering a Prime Minister's wife, was prematurely halted with his arrest on a Pacific island.

Big fat phoney... Arthur Orton was an obese, coarse, semi-literate butcher – yet he briefly succeeded in convincing one of Britain's most aristocratic families that he was the long-lost heir to their title and fortune.

The 'Tichborne Claimant'... Claiming to be the missing Sir Roger Tichborne, Arthur Orton sailed to England from Australia and came within a hair's breadth of succeeding in one of the most far-fetched frauds of all time.

new home in Kensington. She even sent her chauffeur to top peoples' store Harrods to buy fillet steak for her dog Jeeves.

It was incredible that no one ever delved too deeply into Rosemary's spending. But if they did, she had an answer for that too. 'I'm an heiress,' she would reply coyly. 'I have an inheritance of £20 million.' No one disbelieved her. Hospital charity chairman John Young said Rosemary had a royal air about her and a 'great presence'. The fake Lady Aberdour would even cheekily arrive for work in her chauffeur-driven Bentley, regally waving at Mr Young.

There was no end to the fake lady's cheek. She wrote to Richard Stevens enclosing a cheque for £100,000 which, she said, was her gift towards a new hospital ward and adding that her trust fund had given her permission to make donations totalling £500,000 towards this worthy cause over five years. Rosemary asked that her donation be received 'anonymously'. This was hardly surprising when she had stolen the money from a charity headed by Mr Stevens himself.

Rosemary loved the high life. There was no limit to her spending. She would go on wild sprees with her credit cards and think nothing of disposing of £30,000 on a weekend shopping jaunt. She also acquired a new circle of friends, people she felt would not question her aristocratic status too closely. She became renowned for her extravagant parties. As a supposed member of the aristocracy, a respected socialite and now a generous benefactor, she entertained lavishly. One party at her London home had a Caribbean theme. She employed professional party organisers to make sure every attention was paid to detail. Guests, wearing grass skirts and Caribbean shirts, arrived to find live lobsters in tanks of water, bars with Caribbean roofs made out of specially imported materials, two tons of sand, palm trees and champagne spouting from showers. It had taken seven days to 'build' the party, at a cost of £40,000. As one partygoer said: 'It was Rosemary living a dream. It was her going to the Caribbean for the weekend.'

Rosemary was never to explain why she decided upon 'Lady Aberdour' as her aristocratic pseudonym. But there was one particular family who felt she had a lot of explaining to do –

the genuinely titled Aberdours. They only became aware of an impostor when a Sunday newspaper wrote about Rosemary. The writer thought it too audacious to question her face-to-face about her illustrious roots, so he looked the family up in the aristocrats' directory Debretts, found the Aberdours and placed Rosemary as being the twenty-first daughter of the Earl of Morton. The Countess and Earl of Morton were concerned that their family name was being taken in vain and wrote to the *Sunday Times* to tell them so. They were no less anxious when they received a reply saying that there was obviously another branch of the family. 'We were slightly annoyed,' said the countess. 'It was a silly reply. There is no one in the family called Lady Rosemary Aberdour.' The countess's son, Lord Aberdour, added: 'There is only one Lady Aberdour, and that's my wife Amanda. This woman is definitely a fraud.' Yet even when the real Lord and Lady Aberdour found out that someone was living a lie and using their name, no one pursued investigations which would have revealed Rosemary's barefaced fraud.

It was now taking all Rosemary's nerve, not only to maintain her fake existence, but to avoid discovery over rapidly dwindling charity funds at the National Hospital. A scheduled visit from auditors meant Rosemary had to put in overtime to balance the books. She had to adjust figures, produce forged documents and transfer cash. She even raised an overdraft on the Queen's Ball account. The auditors did not notice anything amiss. 'It was all done with stunning skill,' said John Young, who was again to fall victim of Rosemary's quick-thinking. She forged his signature to get her hands on even more cash and, when a building society manager queried it, she told them that 'poor Mr Young' suffered from Parkinson's disease which made his hands shake.

By now, Rosemary knew deep inside that all the money in the world could not buy love or friends. She had no real companions, just hangers-on, and even they were beginning to tire of the party merry-go-round. It was always the same crowd of people, the same old Rosemary determined to put on a party more outrageous than the last and desperate to be the centre of attention. It was a sad fact that guests at some of her parties now mainly comprised staff and the most casual of acquaintances 'She left all her parties early,' said one partygoer, Hamish Mitchell. 'It was as if she wasn't having a good time.'

Ever blinkered to the harsher reality of life, poor little rich girl Rosemary decided to cheer herself up with the biggest party ever. In fact, it was a fortnight of parties. The venue for the two weeks of total self-indulgence was Thornton Watlass Hall, a magnificent country estate in Yorkshire. Every night, the guests sat down to a gourmet dinner. There was live entertainment by top cabaret artists, firework displays, vintage car races and, of course, the best champagne, permanently flowing.

Perhaps living such a complex lie began to take its toll on Rosemary or perhaps she at last realised that the good life would come to an end. Whatever her reasoning, she was determined to give up her 'career' with as much extravagance as she had pursued it. She rented a £123,000-a-year London penthouse with its own swimming pool which was to be the venue for yet more of her flamboyant hospitality. Then she embarked upon the spending spree of a lifetime. There were two £40,000 parties – first a Star Trek Voyage of Discovery Party which Rosemary hosted, followed by a friend's birthday party which took the form of a mediaeval banquet at Conwy Castle in Wales: guests were flown in by helicopter. Then there was the Teddy Bears' Picnic party which cost £70,000 to stage at top London hotel Claridges. Other personal indulgences included a £9,000 'RUA' personalised car number plate for her Mercedes sports car, £78,000 to hire a yacht, £34,000 worth of vintage champagne and £54,000 on her favourite flowers, white lilies. At the height of Rosemary's frenzied spending in December 1990, she was getting through £15,000 every day. In just three months, she spent £1,350,000. By April 1991, Rosemary had all but exhausted the charity donations. For the first time, she began to owe people money.

A few weeks later, Rosemary knew it was all over. Charity director Richard Stevens found a letter in one of Rosemary's office drawers. It bore the forged signatures of both himself and John Young. The letter was to the Abbey National Building

Society, asking them to transfer £250,000. 'It was a very good forgery,' admitted Mr Young. He confronted Rosemary who, cool to the last, told him she had 'cash-flow' problems and that the matter would be sorted out that very afternoon. It never was; Rosemary boarded a plane for Brazil and people started having serious doubts about their socialite friend and devoted charity worker. As Mr Young was to say later: 'The alarm bells rang.' Soon the swindling impostor, who had stolen around £3 million of charity funds, was headline news.

After a week in Rio contemplating her fate, Rosemary was persuaded by her family and boyfriend Michael Cubbin to return to face the music, and she flew back to London to give herself up to the police. Six months on remand followed – during which time she had to get used to a new title 'Prisoner Aberdour, number TT184' – before Rosemary appeared in court to plead guilty to seventeen charges, including five of theft and eleven of obtaining property by deception. She had stolen and spent over £2,700,000. Prosecuting barrister Brendan Finucane said Rosemary's spending had become an addiction. 'She spent all the money on such a grand scale,' he said. 'It was like the compulsion of a gambler. The money all went. She needed to fuel her fantasies and continued to do it until, by chance, she was stopped.'

Rosemary was sentenced to four years in prison. Newspaper reports labelled her 'Snooty Big Spender', 'The Girl Who Tried to Buy Love' and 'Phoney Aristocrat'. And the Essex girl returned to Essex to serve her time, at Bullwood Hall Prison. Meanwhile, the National Hospital was left to sort out the monumental financial fraud she had perpetrated. Managers of the National Hospital Development Fund and the Queen's Square fund refused to accept the mess had been of their making. They blamed building societies and banks for failing to act the moment suspicions had been aroused. Under threat of legal action, the building societies involved paid back £1.5 million pounds, the banks nearly £1 million. The charity was determined to recoup as much of its loss as was humanely possibly, serving writs on those who had provided services or goods in return for their stolen money and fraudulent cheques. As one party organiser said: 'It all got pretty nasty.'

Rosemary's furniture and paintings went back to the shops that had sold them and the money was refunded. Other possessions fetched around £100,000 at a sale organised by London auction house Christie's.

The Charity Commission was called in to investigate how it had all been allowed to happen. Its findings were simple: Rosemary had used charity donations to her own benefit, apparently answerable to no one. And her cunning accountancy meant auditors had failed to notice any discrepancies. National Hospital Development Fund director Richard Stevens left to become a fund-raiser for Southampton University. Chairman John Young survived the scandal and became president of the fund. He later said: 'We shall never know how much Rosemary's fraud was planned. But she took people into her confidence and conned everyone, including her friends, family and fiancé. She was very cunning.' Rosemary was directly responsible for the passing of a new law concerning charity money; the 1992 Cheques Act meaning such forgery supposedly became impossible.

Rosemary served two years of her sentence and was released in October 1993. The National Hospital's long-awaited new wing, with its eight wards, opened three months later. Fiancé Michael Cubbin, a helicopter pilot, stood by Rosemary. They made their home in a village in Oxfordshire. Rosemary was lucky to have a man like Michael as all her so-called friends had deserted her. Promises of million-pound book and film deals about her life had long gone away. The party really was over.

Michael and Rosemary married in November 1994. The wedding took place at Rosemary's local church, back home in Wickham Bishops. The former 'Lady' may not have been able to buy love but, from her bizarre, double-life, she had found it. At 32 years of age, Rosemary had finally found a satisfyingly normal, honest life.

CHAPTER 18

Story of the 'Invisible' Man

To the world outside his sanitised hotel suite, Howard Hughes was the 'Invisible Man', a recluse who had hidden himself from prying eyes for decades. At various stages of his life a daredevil aviator, a womaniser, an oil tycoon, an industrialist and a Hollywood mogul, he was rich beyond imagination. Yet by the 1970s he had chosen to live out his last days as a sad, obsessed hermit in self-imposed imprisonment and hidden from the light of day.

The contrast between his former life and his present existence, guarded by a sinister set of Mormon minders, caused him to be a figure of media rumour and deep public fascination. So one can understand the excitement of a publishing house when it was offered the 'authorised biography' of this bizarre billionaire, written with the co-operation of Hughes himself.

It was labelled 'the literary coup of the century' and warranted spectacular rewards for the author of the work, Clifford Irving, who successfully demanded a record advance from American publishers McGraw-Hill. The only problem was that the 'authorised biography' was no such thing. Howard Hughes had never met Clifford Irving. He hadn't even heard of him – though he soon would.

The man who became infamous as the 'Howard Hughes Hoaxer' hit on his extraordinary plot in 1970 when he read an article about Hughes in *Newsweek* magazine. Entitled 'The Case of the Invisible Billionaire', it reported that Hughes had shut himself away from the outside world and that he was in such ill health that he no longer had proper control of his business empire.

Irving, an American expatriate living on the Mediterranean island of Ibiza, put down the magazine and pondered how he could take advantage of the fact that the ex-playboy, reputed to be the world's richest man, was now such a living fossil. He began to research his subject.

The last time Hughes had been interviewed had been in 1958. Since then, he had become a mystery man, never being seen in public, never speaking to anyone outside his household. So, mused Irving, if no one could get to speak to him, then how could they discover a proposed biography on him was fake?

Irving put the idea to his friend Dick Suskind. They agreed to work as a team, fabricating interviews with Hughes, offering the book to a publisher and even forging Hughes' signature on papers 'agreeing' to the project.

Irving was already an expert on faking and forgery; he had won some acclaim for his book *Fake!* exposing the work of art forger Elmyr de Hory. His initial approach to New York-based McGraw-Hill was to say that he had sent a copy of *Fake!* to Hughes and had received a letter of thanks. He asked the publishers if they knew of any forthcoming books about the billionaire recluse.

Knowing something more was needed to whet McGraw-Hill's appetite, he included letters addressed to him 'in Hughes's handwriting' suggesting interest in a book about his life. Irving had practised forging the tycoon's handwriting for many hours, having seen a photograph of it accompanying the article in *Newsweek* magazine. His expertise encouraged him to pen longer and longer letters, one of them nine pages long.

In one of them, Hughes supposedly wrote: 'It would not suit me to die without having certain misconceptions about my life cleared up and without having stated the truth about my life. I would be grateful if you would let me know when and how you would wish to undertake the writing of my biography you proposed.'

An amazing coincidence then occurred which could have ended Irving's hoax there and then. On a visit to McGraw-Hill's offices, he was told that a letter from Hughes had appeared in another publication, *Life* magazine. The publishers had taken a quick glance at it and immediately become reassured that the letters sent to Irving were indeed genuine. Irving rushed away to buy a copy of the magazine – and was astonished to see that Howard Hughes' handwriting in the reproduced letter was nothing like that he had forged in his letters. It was incredible that McGraw-Hill had not made a direct comparison.

By virtue of the *Life* magazine letter, however, Irving now had an even better sample of Hughes' handwriting to copy. This he did with another two letters supposedly addressed to him from the billionaire. They too were sent to McGraw-Hill. Again, no one thought to compare the second batch of Hughes letters with the first. If they had, they could not have helped but spot the differences in handwriting styles.

Irving added one extra enticement to McGraw-Hill, giving them details of phone calls he said he had received from Hughes. The publishers were firmly hooked. The company's vice-president Albert Leventhal offered Irving a contract giving him $100,000 on signature, $100,000 on delivery of the transcript of interviews and $300,000 for the biography manuscript. It was December 7, 1971, and McGraw-Hill announced its intention to publish the exclusive Howard Hughes biography on March 27, 1972.

Such a deal seemed to demonstrate extreme naivety on the part of such an established company. No one questioned how Irving had managed to bypass Rosemont Enterprise Inc – the company the Hughes organisation had set up to make illegal the use or reproduction by anyone but Rosemont of the name Howard Hughes. And no one queried how Irving had suddenly become a close confidant of the billionaire when he had never even mentioned his name before. McGraw-Hill, however, saw no reason to doubt Irving's sincerity. They had been the publishers of *Fake!* and now their loyal author was offering them what could possibly be the final account of Hughes' life in the words of the man himself.

Irving's book deal included several provisos: that only top executives of the company should know about the project and that there must be no attempt to contact Hughes. Only Irving had his trust. And so sensitive was the book that it should be given the code name *Senor Octavio*. Further, not a single soul outside of the select few should be told about the book.

Meanwhile, McGraw-Hill began capitalising on its investment. The company sold serial rights of the forthcoming biography to *Life* magazine for $250,000. The contract stated that if Hughes withdrew his authorisation of the biography at any date, that money would have to be repaid.

Word, of course, soon got out about the 'publishing coup of the century'. The Howard Hughes empire, in the form of his public relations firm, were thrown into confusion about the proposed book, as were a vast number of journalists. It was the first they had heard of it. All attempts to contact Hughes himself were blocked, as ever. Approaches made to his public relations company about an impending biography were met with firm denial. But this just made journalists more convinced the book existed; the Hughes organisation always denied anything about their master.

At this point of the hoax, Irving believed that it was all a bit of fun and he could throw the plot into reverse if he so chose. He said later: 'It seemed like such an elegant act, and one from which I could withdraw at any time if I wanted. That was the great fallacy.' Irving and Dick Suskind claimed they were sucked into the hoax and then locked into the fraud.

The duplicitous duo started researching Howard Hughes in earnest. They acquired every single scrap of information they could about the man but soon realised that writing a book which appeared to have had the full co-operation of their subject was a monumental task. Here fate dealt Irving a staggering piece of luck.

An old acquaintance, Stanley Meyer, contacted Irving with news of an existing, half-finished book about Hughes. It had been written by a journalist, James Phelan, in conjunction with a former employee and true confidante of Hughes, Noah Dietrich. The agent for the book had been none other than Irving's old friend Meyer.

Author Phelan and agent Meyer had parted company after the manuscript had been blocked by Hughes' mighty legal team. But that did not stop Stanley Meyer passing a copy of the uncompleted manuscript to Irving, who photocopied every page before handing it back.

Irving was now able to inform McGraw-Hill that so successful were his interviews with Hughes that the book was developing into an autobiography, written almost first-hand by the subject himself. And contrary to rumours that Hughes was no longer mentally alert, he was in fact so wily that he was demanding an even bigger fee for his time and trouble. He wanted $850,000.

The money, as originally agreed, was to be paid into the Zurich bank account of one H. R. Hughes. McGraw-Hill was on the point of refusing a bigger payment – until it heard a rival biography on Hughes was being prepared by another publishing house.

It was only a matter of time before Howard Hughes himself decided to take a stand over the growing number of books all claiming to have been written with his authorisation. The recluse gave his first press conference for more than fifteen years. The telephone link-up organised between Hughes in Palm Beach, Florida, and journalists in a Los Angeles studio was hot with denial. Hughes did not know anyone called Clifford Irving; he had not met anyone called Clifford Irving.

Irving tried one last desperate attempt to save himself. He said the voice talking to the reporters was not that of Hughes but that of an impostor. His protestations failed – and the cracks in his story began to open up when James Phelan discovered that Irving's authorised biography was stolen from his own work and produced his manuscript to prove it.

Next, McGraw-Hill officially filed a complaint with the Swiss authorities to investigate the Swiss bank account. But it was a detective agency called in by Hughes himself which discovered that 'H.R. Hughes' was in fact a woman. She was called Helga and she made frequent visits to the bank to withdraw large amounts of money. That woman was Irving's wife Edith.

Edith Irving not only suffered the shock of being exposed; the exhaustive investigations into her husband's exploits revealed that on the occasions when he had told her he was travelling the world to set up the hoax, he was actually in the arms of other women.

Clifford and Edith Irving and Dick Suskind appeared before two Grand Jury hearings on February 7 and March 3, 1972. They all confessed to their elaborate fraud. Between them, they owed more than $1,500,000 to McGraw-Hill, the taxman and their lawyers. Irving received a thirty-month jail sentence and Suskind six months. Enid Irving had twenty-two months of her two-year sentence suspended only to receive another two-year sentence in Zurich for her fraudulent banking habits.

An autobiography on Howard Hughes never did hit the bookstands. The eccentric billionaire died on April 5, 1976. At least that was the date given. Such was the secrecy surrounding Hughes at the end of his days that no one can be sure of the circumstances of his death.

On release from jail, Irving teamed up once again with Dick Suskind. Together they wrote *Project Octavio*, the story of how they schemed to pull off the biggest publishing coup of the century.

Three decades after the death of Howard Hughes, the story was retold, this time as a movie, *The Hoax*, with Richard Gere playing the part of Clifford Irving. At the time of its release in 2007, the real Irving was persuaded to talk again about his astonishing literary coup. The master hoaxer, by now 76, married to his sixth wife and living modestly in Aspen, Colorado, explained how he became mired in such a web of deceit:

'We thought it was just a hoax. They can't put you in jail for a hoax, can they? Especially as we still had the money to give back, as we did. I thought I'd be stopped somewhere along the line at an early stage. But then we had a run of such wonderful luck with the project that we just sank deeper and deeper into the quicksand. It's a long time ago – and I paid the price.'

CHAPTER 19

Fortune of Bricks and Straw

hérèse Humbert had learned one simple truth in life: that the world is full of gullible people who will believe anything if it is repeated often enough. And although she was no beauty – the French provincial washerwoman was as podgy as she was penniless – she had a certain magnetism that would win over the rich and famous. Her charismatic attraction would also win her the hand in marriage of a trusting husband and ultimately make her a fortune.

Thérèse was born in 1860 to peasant farmer Gilbert Aurignac and grew up hearing the endless repetition of her father's fanciful stories of his elevated ancestry. Neglecting his fields, Aurignac would spend idle days in the cafés of the small town of Beauzelle, drinking himself into a stupor on cheap red wine while regaling his fellow drinkers with the unlikely tales of his family's former glory – how his real name was d'Aurignac and how he had been disowned by his aristocratic father. But, he said, his two sons and two daughters would inherit vast wealth upon his death. Aurignac's oldest child, Thérèse, believed every word of it – until her braggart father's death. Only then did she learn the truth: that she, her sister and two brothers had been left paupers and she would have to take in washing to keep the family fed.

Thérèse's next humble steps in life led her to the nearest city, Toulouse, where she went to work as a laundry maid at the home of the mayor, an ambitious lawyer and politician named Gustave Humbert. There she began to employ the inventive talents that she had learned from her father – but to much greater effect. First, she allowed herself to be seduced by her boss's son, Frederic, to whom she wove the most astonishing story. As a youngster, she said, she had attracted the attention of a rich spinster named Mademoiselle de

Marcotte. Now very old and without any surviving relatives, this venerable lady had written a will bequeathing to Thérèse her entire estate, including its chateau and vineyards.

Frederic believed every word of her tale, fell madly in love with her and, despite the protestations of his father, secretly married her. He took her to Paris, where he launched a career as an advocate. The fees he earned, however, were wholly insufficient to sustain the extraordinary spending of his ex-washerwoman wife. She fell in love with 'Gay Paree' and entered into the social whirl. On the back of her 'inheritance' the couple borrowed more and more money – until one day their creditors checked on the identity of her benefactor and found there was no such person as Mademoiselle de Marcotte.

There were several things that Thérèse could have done. She could have fled the city. She could have stuck to her story. She could have owned up to her fraud. Or she could simply pile fresh lies upon the old ones. Thérèse chose the latter course; her story about Mademoiselle de Marcotte had indeed been untrue, she said, but she had fabricated the tale only to disguise the true identity of her benefactor. He was Robert Henry Crawford, a millionaire American from Chicago, whom she had met on a train two years previously. They had become friends and, when he subsequently suffered a heart attack, she had nursed him back to health. Mr Crawford had since died, however, and had left his fortune to be shared between his two nephews in the United States and Thérèse's younger sister Marie. Marie, then still a schoolgirl, would not receive her inheritance until she was 21 years of age but in the meantime Thérèse was to receive an annual income of just under $100,000.

One of the people to whom Thérèse told this fresh pack of lies was her father-in-law, Gustave Humbert. The Toulouse mayor had risen rapidly in the world of politics and was now Minister of Justice in the national government. Whether or not he believed Thérèse's tale, she nevertheless persuaded him to pay all her and Frederic's Paris creditors to avoid a family scandal. In turn, she 'repaid' old Monsieur Humbert by publicly announcing that the documents containing her inheritance had been placed by American lawyers in a locked safe, the administration and secure keeping of which had been guaranteed by the Humbert family until her sister Marie came of age.

As Paris buzzed with the story of the 'Crawford Inheritance', Thérèse boldly turned up at the bank to which she had previously owed the most money. Warmly welcomed by the manager, she told him: 'Sadly, Monsieur, I am not permitted to open the safe and exercise the bonds and securities therein until Marie comes of age. Otherwise, I am in danger of forfeiting all claim upon the Crawford millions.'

Predictably, she then asked for a loan. It was readily given. Thérèse repeated the trick at banks throughout Paris and elsewhere. One Toulouse bank alone advanced her seven million francs. Much of the money was used to purchase a lavish mansion in the capital, in her bedroom she installed a safe supposedly containing the secrets of her and her little sister's fortune.

The door of this massive, fireproof, steel structure was opened only once, when she invited an over-awed provincial notary to examine a number of bundles of paper and to itemise the wrappers that supposedly indicated their contents. Then the safe was locked and thick wax seals were applied to the doors and handles. The imposing safe was not to be opened again until Marie's twenty-first birthday.

Meanwhile, Thérèse and Frederic embarked on an unprecedented spending spree. Thérèse also invited sister Marie and their two brothers, Emile and Romain, to join her in an orgy of extravagance. The human cash-dispenser became known in Paris society as 'La Grande Thérèse', as the ample-bosomed lady swept in and out of restaurants and fashion salons and opera boxes.

Only one mishap threatened their idyll. A Lyon banker named Delatte visited Thérèse at her Paris mansion to arrange the advance of a further loan secured on the inheritance. Idly, he inquired where in America her late benefactor had lived. Off the top of her head, Thérèse replied: 'Somerville, a suburb of Boston.' Unbeknown to Thérèse, the Lyon banker was about to sail to the United States and, while in Boston, made enquiries about the fictitious millionaire James Henry

Crawford. Discovering that no one had ever heard of such a person, Monsieur Delatte wrote to a fellow banker in France telling him of his suspicions.

Before further investigations could be made in the United States, however, Delatte mysteriously vanished. After a few days, his body was fished out of the East River, New York. He had been murdered. The killer was never uncovered but it has always been assumed that Delatte's untimely death was what would now be known as a 'contract killing', ordered by Thérèse or her brothers. And it took only the glib tongue of 'La Grande Thérèse' to calm the fears of the French banker to whom Delatte had written. The threat of exposure evaporated, as did the money that the Humbert clan continued to borrow, which had now reached an estimated 65 million francs.

There was one event that Thérèse Humbert could not influence, however: the twenty-first birthday of sister Marie. The day was looming like a time bomb ticking away inside the great safe. Thérèse countered with two plans. The first was to distract attention from the vital birthday by inventing a dispute between herself and the non-existent American nephews over where the securities should be stored. Her second ploy was for her brothers to establish a finance house in a rented building in fashionable Boulevard des Capucines and to seek investment business through a chain of salesmen. Early investors found their returns swift and satisfactorily high, and the money flowed in. None of it was invested, of course. Apart from the small sums paid out in high 'interest', the rest was put aside to reimburse some of the more pressing creditors who wanted their loans repaid the moment Marie came of age.

The whole corrupt edifice began to collapse when a Bank of France official, Jules Bizat, investigated the invested funds of the Humbert brothers' finance house and found that there were none. He went straight to the Prime Minister, Pierre Marie Waldeck-Rousseau. Fearing that official involvement would precipitate yet another governmental scandal (there had already been several at the close of the Nineteenth Century) the Premier decided to leak the story to the Paris newspaper *Le Matin*. Thérèse had no alternative but to protest her innocence while fending off the demands of creditors.

Now began an extraordinary chain of events. The Humberts' lawyer, Maitre du Buit, believed so fervently in the truth of the Crawford inheritance that he threatened to sue the newspaper for libel and offered to open the safe to clear her name. This was the very last thing that Thérèse wanted, of course, and she panicked. On May 8, 1902, two days before the safe was due to be opened by du Buit, Thérèse or one of her accomplices set fire to the upper floor of her home. Everything in her bedroom was gutted, apart from the safe, which proved itself totally fireproof.

Thérèse, now enmeshed in a web of her own lies, assembled her sister, her brothers and husband Frederic, and took a train to an unknown destination. Thus, she was nowhere to be found when, on the appointed day, lawyer du Buit led an anxious band of businessmen and bankers into Thérèse's bedroom. The wax seals were broken, the doors were unlocked and eager hands swung them back to reveal... a single house brick!

Many years earlier, upon the death of Thérèse's boastful father Gilbert Aurignac, his children had stood around as Madame Aurignac turned the key in an old oak chest which, he had long boasted, contained papers documenting the family's secret fortune. It too had contained nothing but a brick. Now Thérèse was repeating history, though for a much more august company.

The aftermath of the discovery in her bedroom safe in 1902 reverberated around the social and financial circles of France. Ten suicides were attributed to her fraudulent machinations, one of them that of a leading banker. But of the lady herself, there was no sign. Thérèse and her family remained undetected for seven months until Spanish police traced them to a Madrid lodging house. They were extradited and, in February 1903, she, Frederic, Emile and Romain were sent for trial on no fewer than 257 charges of forgery and fraud. On August 8 they stood in the dock at the Palais de Justice while, outside the court, queues formed of thousands of spectators from all over France.

Special trains had even been laid on, such was the fascination for this 'trial of the century'. They were disappointed to see that the arch trickster, 'La Grande Thérèse', was by now just a plump, sallow old woman whose once-magnetic personality had seemingly deserted her. A foreign newsman disparagingly called her 'a typical French cook'. Thérèse and Frederic were each sentenced to five years in prison. Romain got three years and Emile two.

After the trial, the famous brick, along with the charred metal safe surrounding it, went on display in a Paris shop window where it became something of a tourist attraction. Thérèse herself was released after three and a half years because of her good conduct in jail. She hid herself away in the countryside, living in obscurity and relative poverty until 1917 when, overshadowed by the horrors of the First World War, she died, her passing unreported and her deeds largely forgotten.

CHAPTER 20

'Antiques' of the Artful Codger

He certainly looked genuine enough. An old man in a wheelchair rather pitifully selling off the family heirlooms. The story was always the same. The precious items had been found in the attic or inherited in a recent will. In truth, everything about 84-year-old George Greenhalgh was false.

Far from being a needy pensioner fallen on hard times, Greenhalgh was undertaking a string of forgeries – a highly dodgy business that earned him the nickname 'the Artful Codger'. And when he masqueraded as a rather confused old man asking if the items he was offering had any value, he knew of course that they did not.

But at least Greenhalgh had not stolen any of the property he was selling. It all came from the creative talents of his son Shaun, working away in his garden shed – talents that fooled prestigious art houses and museums for eighteen years. Also in on the scam were George's wife Olive and son George Jr, who handled money matters.

The Artful Codger and his son did not always get away with it, as a court was later to hear, but a series of circumstances meant they still enjoyed a very rewarding career until they were found out.

In 1989, George Greenhalgh tried to sell a Tenth Century Anglo-Saxon silver vessel, the 'Eadred Reliquary', to Manchester University. He said he had found it while out with his metal detector in a park in Preston. The university doubted its authenticity.

In 1990, Peter Nahum, an international art dealer from The Leicester Galleries, in London's St James's, took a call from Greenhalgh's wife, Olive, who wanted to sell a still life by Samuel Peploe which she had apparently inherited from her grandfather. But it was her husband who arrived with the painting late one afternoon and insisted on cash, saying the rival Portland Gallery might be interested.

Feeling under pressure to make a quick decision, Mr Nahum handed over a cheque for £20,000. Later that night, he took a closer look at the painting and asked for the opinion of his art restorer, Hamish Dewar. Both men declared it a clever fake.

The next day, Mr Nahum faxed Scotland Yard's art and antiques squad to pass on the information. Sadly for the art world, this information did not get processed. A former detective sergeant was some years later to confess the squad was understaffed at the time.

The following year, 1991, George Greenhalgh introduced himself to Peter Clayton, of Seaby's Antiquities, in London's Old Bond Street. Clayton later recalled how a grey-haired, balding man wearing spectacles arrived at the gallery carrying a suitcase 'He seemed like an ordinary, elderly gent,' Mr Clayton said. 'He was bluff and amiable, like a farmer.' Inside the suitcase, wrapped in a tartan blanket, was a silver tray which Greenhalgh said was a family treasure. It was a clever replica of a Roman silver tray known as the 'Risley Park Lanx' which had been lost from stately home Risley Park, found by a ploughman in 1729, only to disappear again.

After quite intense analysis, two British Museum experts agreed it was 'probably a copy', though not a recent one, and could even have been made using the original metal. The tray was bought by a dealer for £100,000 and later put on display at the British Museum. Here, yet more experts examined the piece, remembered the Greenhalgh name and then contacted the art and antiques squad. Again, the response was that the department had too much work on to look at the case.

In 1995, George Greenhalgh tried to sell an Anglo-Saxon ring through Phillips Auctioneers, who took it to the British Museum for analysis. The keeper of the European pre-history department decided it was 'of modern origin' – in other words, a copy created only recently.

Yet another chance to expose the Greenhalghs came in 1999 when Christie's was asked for an opinion on two Roman gold ornaments. They were withdrawn from sale after the bespectacled old man refused to allow them to be scientifically analysed. Once more, suspicious art experts checked their records, which showed that Greenhalgh had links with a number of fakes in the past.

None of this stopped the 2003 sale of one of the Greenhalgh family's pride and joys, the Amarna Princess – even though Christie's, when asked to value it, expressed concerns about its history. George Greenhalgh was as convincing as ever, maintaining the pretence that he knew little about any item he wanted to sell by saying he thought the statue would make a nice garden ornament.

The Amarna Princess caused ripples throughout the art world. It was a voluptuous, headless statue of one of the six daughters of Pharaoh Akhenaten and Queen Nefertiti (mother of the legendary Tutankhamun), carved out of translucent alabaster. The 20-inch figure was thought to date back to 1350 BC. Those who saw it noted it was more impressive than the other statue of its kind in the Louvre gallery in Paris.

The princess, in the Egyptian Armana style, was sold to Bolton Council for £440,000, paid for largely out of public funds. In 2004, after first being exhibited at London's Hayward Gallery, it took pride of place in Bolton Museum, which boasted it had got a bargain. Keepers felt the figure was worth £1 million. They also believed the story of the anonymous seller of the statue, who claimed it came into his family when it was bought by a relative at a sale of items at Silverton Park, Devon, home to the Fourth Earl of Egremont in 1892.

It was, said Angela Thomas, the Keeper of Egyptology, 'a rare piece of great significance'. In fact, it had taken Shaun Greenhalgh just three weeks to make the statue out of clay in his shed, using tea as a coating. Angela Thomas was somewhat astray in her opinion of George Greenhalgh as being 'a nice old man'.

This sale was a turning point for George and his son. A bust of Thomas Jefferson allegedly sculpted by Greenhalgh – but actually manufactured in their workshop in the garden of their modest end-of-terraced council home in a Bolton suburb – sold at Sotheby's for £48,000. A 'Barbara Hepworth' terracotta goose was bought by the Henry Moore Institute for £3,000.

Another of Shaun Greenhalgh's forgeries was a 'Gaugin' pottery faun bought by the Chicago Institute of Art, which featured it in an international touring exhibition. Visitors were told in the exhibition catalogue to note the object's 'phallic tail... an iconography linked to Gaugin's failing relationship with his wife'.

It is believed the family made at least £850,000 through their forgeries, though police said £1 million was probably a more accurate figure. If they had sold all 120 items that had been created in the garden shed, they could have made more than £10 million.

Throughout their reign of forgery, the family made approaches to many illustrious institutions. As well as the British Museum, Manchester Museum, Christie's and Sotheby's, they had dealings with the Tate and Tate Modern, the Henry Moore Museum in Leeds, Chester, Liverpool, Ireland and Dresden museums and auctioneers Bonham's and Phillips.

In all, the list of copied artists included painters L S Lowry and Samuel Peploe, sculptures from Barbara Hepworth, Henry Moore, Otto Dix, Horatio Greenough, Man Ray, Brancusi and Gaugin. 'Antiques' included Roman silver and gold artefacts, with original metals probably from coins, Assyrian stone reliefs and Anglo-Saxon jewellery.

None, of course, came from great homes, wealthy relatives or bequests but from the red-brick terraced house on an estate close to the west Pennine moors in the north Bolton suburb of Bromley Cross.

When the family's exposure finally came, experts confessed they were impressed by Shaun Greenhalgh's ability to re-create some great works of art. Although lacking in education – he left school at 16 with no qualifications – he painstakingly read up on history, art and antiques, gleaning all the information he needed to make his own. He became an acceptable self-taught artist, once boasting he could run-off a Turner-inspired Moran watercolour in half-an-hour.

During his 'practice' for his future career, Shaun had attempted a wide range of crafts from painting in pastels and watercolours to sketches and sculpture, both modern and ancient, from busts and statues to bas-relief and metal work. He invested in a vast range of different materials, such as silver, stone, marble, rare stone, replica metal and glass. He also carried out meticulous research to authenticate his items with histories and provenance, such as faking letters from the supposed artists. One neighbour was later to relate how Shaun was a bit of a tearaway, often throwing what appeared to be broken old plates around the garden. Sometimes ancient coins were seen in a hedge.

It was inevitable, however, that mistakes would be made by the Greenhalghs. And that would be their downfall.

Three Assyrian marble reliefs said to date back to the ninth and seventh century BC were valued at £250,000 but the British Museum spotted a spelling mistake in the inscription – and that the horses were wearing Twentieth Century harnesses. The stone they were carved in came from Wiltshire. George Greenhalgh had written to the British Museum enclosing photographs of the three reliefs in the Assyrian style. Unaware of the growing file on the Greenhalghs, a member of staff at the museum was immediately excited, particularly as one of the reliefs, of a soldier and horses, appeared to be from the 'palace of Sennacherib in Nineveh'. 'A superb example,' wrote John Curtis, keeper of the Middle East department at the museum.

Not long afterwards, Shaun Greenhalgh took the items to the museum, which bought the horse relief. The other two went for sale at Bonham's where they were examined by Chantelle Waddington, head of antiquities, and consultant Richard Falkiner, who later said: 'It was a gut instinct, but stylistically, it didn't add up.' He added: 'I took one look at the relief and said, "Don't make me laugh". It was an obvious fake. It was far too freshly cut, was made of the wrong stone and was stylistically wrong for the period.'

Richard Falkiner and Chantelle Waddington contacted the British Museum, where staff began a more detailed forensic examination. Scotland Yard experts, at last finding the resources to get on to the Artful Codger case, found themselves involved in what would later become a parody of the BBC television programme *The Antiques Road Show* – 'The Antiques Rogue Show'.

The police team who raided the Greenhalgh's home were amazed at the cottage industry set up behind the closed doors. Said one: 'There were blocks of stone, a furnace for melting silver on top of the fridge, half-finished and rejected sculptures, a watercolour under the bed, a cheque for £20,000 dated 1993 and a bust of an American president in the loft. I'd never seen anything like it.'

In 2007, Shaun Greenhalgh, then 47, and his mother Olive, 83, were found guilty at Bolton Crown Court of conspiring to defraud the arts and antiques world with the sale of forged work between 1989 and 2006. At the centre of the case were 44 known forgeries. On November 16 of that year, Shaun was sent to prison for four-and-a-half years and Olive was given a twelve-month suspended sentence.

It was Olive Greenhalgh who had made the initial phone calls to potential buyers because Shaun was 'shy and did not like to use the telephone'. The police suggested Shaun was motivated less by profit than by resentment at his own lack of recognition as an artist. This 'general hatred' became a real need to 'shame the art world and show them up'.

Defence lawyer Andrew Nutall characterised Shaun as a shy, introverted person, obsessed with 'one outlook and that was his garden shed'. The forgeries were an attempt to 'perfect the love he had for such arts. By implication, the forgeries were a mere unintended, if unfortunate, consequence'.

On January 28, 2008, George Greenhalgh, 84, was given a two-year suspended jail sentence. He had admitted conspiracy to defraud art institutions and money-laundering at an earlier hearing, but his case was adjourned when Judge William Morris asked if any jails could 'humanely' imprison a wheelchair-bound pensioner in poor health. The answer was 'no' and Greenhalgh escaped time behind bars. But he heard Judge Morris state: 'You and your son and wife, over a period of sixteen years, conspired together to deceive the art world and the world of antiquities, galleries and museums, auction houses, experts and collectors, both private and public. Yours was a subordinate but very important role in this conspiracy.'

George Greenhalgh Junior was subsequently given a nine-month-suspended sentence and the family were ordered to pay back more than £400,000 in compensation. After sentencing, Detective Constable Con Halina Racki, from the Metropolitan Police's Fine Art Squad, said more unsuspecting collectors may still be in possession of Greenhalgh fakes. The police had managed to recover only twenty.

Andrew Nuttall stated that the Amarna Princess statue should be destroyed along with the other Greenhalgh fakes in case they should disappear and end up on the market again. He rejected prosecution arguments that the forgeries should be kept for use in training and put on display at exhibitions, saying: 'It appears there is a ghoulish celebration of forgery which the art world seems to delight in. The fakes should be consigned to the dustbin of history.'

Scotland Yard described the family as 'possibly the most diverse forgery team in the world, ever'.

Even after the court case, little was known about George Greenhalgh. It was suggested that he had perhaps realised the value of lost treasures when he'd taken up metal detecting as a hobby. He had described his former career as a technical drawing teacher, though no one could find out where he taught. He had served in World War Two and had been wounded in Italy. It was no wonder that the good judge had sympathy for him after hearing Greenhalgh say: 'I got two bullets in my head and one in my back and it still hurts.'

After the trial, many of those who had been duped by the Greenhalghs scrambled to distance themselves from their mistakes. Bolton Museum described itself as 'blameless', insisting that it had followed established procedure. Judge Morris, exonerated the institution and any council staff involved, preferring to focus on what he saw as 'misapplied' talent and an 'ambitious conspiracy', while the Metropolitan Police Arts and Antiquities Unit would only admit that Greenhalgh had succeeded 'to a degree'.

However, the general public was notably more cynical in its reaction, being unimpressed by what they perceived as the experts' incompetence and the law's heavy-handedness. Referring to the Bolton Museum purchase, one local resident commented: 'I like the phrase "subsequently closely examined". Shouldn't this have happened before the £440,000 was paid?'

Just where the money went from the family's prolific efforts is a mystery. Bank records for the family only went back six years, so just how much money passed through their hands will never be known. There were two savings accounts, one containing £55,173 and the other £303,646. Both were frozen.

The Greenhalghs certainly did not live in style. There was only the occasional purchase, such as a new Ford Focus car bought from the proceeds of the Egyptian Princess. Their existence was frugal and they did not even have a computer. They did not go on holidays. It was doubted whether Olive even left Bolton. A neighbour said: 'They kept themselves very much to themselves.' Police could not help but notice the large library of art books, however, and the fact that at a time when the family had so much money in the bank, they continued to draw welfare benefit.

Locally, George Greenhalgh had always been known as something of an artist. Said one neighbour: 'He used to make these lovely stone Greek statues years ago and sell them on the front lawn as garden ornaments. I once said to Olive, "If your husband was dishonest he could be a rich man". She just sort of recoiled with a shocked look on her face.'

A description of known forgeries includes the following:

1989

Eadred Reliquary. A small Tenth Century silver vessel, containing a relic of the true cross of Jerusalem. George Greenhalgh turned up 'dripping wet' at Manchester University, claiming he'd found it in a river terrace at Preston. The university determined the vessel was a fake but was unsure about the wood. Purchased it for £100; the subject of an academic thesis.

1990

Samuel Peploe still life painting, purportedly inherited from Olive's grandfather, sold for £20,000. However, paint began to flake off and buyer cancelled cheque. Scotland Yard failed to make an arrest at the time due to 'organisational restraints'.

Sketch and watercolour acquired by Bolton Museum. 'The former was a gift given by the Greenhalghs; the latter was purchased for £10,000.'

1994

The Faun. A ceramic sculpture by Gauguin. Authenticated by the Wildenstein Institute, sold at Sotheby's auction in 1994 for £20,700 to private London dealers, Howie & Pillar. Bought by the Art Institute of Chicago in 1997 for $125,000. On display until October 2007.

1995

Anglo-Saxon ring. Tried to sell it through Phillips Auctioneers; determined by British Museum to be a fake.

Twenty-four Thomas Moran sketches sold in New York. Possibly of landscapes of Yellowstone Park in the United States. Police believe up to 40, worth up to £10,000, were created by Greenhalgh, six or seven of which are unaccounted for. He claimed each one only took him 30 minutes to forge, and that a former mayor of Bolton had given them to an ancestor of his who worked for the mayor as a cleaner.

1998

The Risley Park Lanx. A Roman silver plate bought for £100,000 by private buyers and donated to the British Museum, which displayed it as genuine replica.

L S Lowry. *The Meeting House*. A pastel, one of a 'clutch of paintings' by Lowry. The Greenhalghs claimed it was a twenty-first birthday present by Olive's gallery owner father, and even that some were gifted by Lowry himself. They had copied letters from the artist, inserting their names in to make it look like they were great friends. For example, this letter dated June 16, 1946:

Dear George, Thank you very much for your recent letter and cheque for the paintings. I have about finished the [*illegible*] but I will hold onto it untill [*sic*] I am ready. I will slip round to the yard on Wed. – L S Lowry. (Received £45.0.0 for paintings.)

One of the Lowrys, perhaps the one mentioned above, sold as a replica for somewhere between £700 and £5,000. Eventually put up for auction by new owners in Kent as genuine item for £70,000.

1999

Two gold Roman ornaments. George Greenhalgh withdrew them from Christies when the auction house wanted to do a scientific analysis on them.

Barbara Hepworth goose sculpture. Only a photograph known to exist before item lost in the late 1920s. The Greenhalghs claimed it was gifted to the family 'by the curator of a museum in Leeds' in the 1950s. Worth approximately £200,000, it was later sold to the Henry Moore Institute in Leeds for £3,000.

Work by Otto Dix. Stolen from Dresden in 1939. Apparently recovered by the Greenhalghs then presented to the Tate Gallery.

Work by Brancusi.

Work by Man Ray.

Another Paul Gaugin, a vase.

Ancient Celtic kilt brooch.

Horatio Greenough. Bust of Thomas Jefferson sold at Sotheby's for £48,000. And/or Thomas Chatterton. Another bust of John Adam. Sold together at Sotheby's for £160,000.

Henry Moore. A carved stone head by Henry Moore, which Greenhalgh Snr tried to convince the Tate Modern, London to buy, claiming to have got it via his grandmother.

2003

Amarna Princess, a statuette. In the family for 'a hundred years'. Authenticated by the British Museum and Sotheby's, bought by Bolton Museum for £440,000, it was on display for three years. A police raid on the Greenhalgh home discovered two more copies.

2005

Three Assyrian marble reliefs from Nineveh, including one of an eagle-headed genie and another of soldiers and horses. They were dated by the British Museum at around 681BC, supposedly from the Palace of Sennacherib, and thought to be worth around £250,000 to £300,000. But alerted by Bonham's, their discrepancies were revealed, and the forgery exposed.

CHAPTER 21

Sincerely Rich, Seriously Crooked

He went from delivery boy to entrepreneur, duping thousands of investors out of their money; from social worker to socialite. When Bernie Cornfeld died in March 1995, he had lived, worked and played hard. But above all, he will forever be known as the big business man who went bust in a spectacular way. Like everything in his life, he did it in style, so it was no surprise that all the newspaper photographs accompanying his obituary showed him with a beaming smile and surrounded by beautiful young women.

Yet, on the face of it, Bernie Cornfeld had little to smile about. He had perpetrated one of the most extraordinarily audacious frauds in history, had been uncovered, disgraced, severely censured and locked up in prison. He had once owned a private jet, a mansion in Beverly Hills, a house in London's Belgravia, and chateaux in France and Switzerland, all bought with other people's money. He never seemed to care a damn about those he defrauded, although he must have felt the loss when the courts removed most of his wealth.

Nor was he very gallant about the women in his life. He once said: 'A beautiful woman with a brain is like a beautiful woman with a club foot.' Yet until his dying day, at the age of 67, Bernie Cornfeld shared his Californian home with eight beautiful women, with two more waiting for his call in London. What was the secret that kept the ugly old fraud smiling to the very end?

Bernie Cornfeld was born in Istanbul on August 17, 1927. His father was a Romanian-Jewish actor and his mother came from a Russian-Jewish family. They moved to America when Cornfeld was four, and two years later his father died. To bring much-needed money into the home, Cornfeld got jobs as a delivery boy and in a fruit store, working after he left school each day. Although he suffered from a stammer, the young lad had a natural gift for selling and when a schoolfriend's father died, the two of them used the $3,000 insurance money to purchase and run an 'age and weight' guessing stand at the Coney Island funfair.

During the Second World War, Cornfeld joined the US Maritime Service (the Training Division of the War Shipping Administration) and afterwards went to Brooklyn College, graduating with a degree in psychology. He then did an MA in social work at the New York School of Social Work, Columbia University. Cornfeld started his working life as a social worker but then switched to selling mutual funds for an investment house. In 1955, he left New York for Paris and, using his savings of a few hundred dollars, set up Investors Overseas Services, the company by which he became famous – or infamous.

Although the IOS headquarters were in Geneva, Switzerland, the main operational base was in Ferney-Voltaire in France, a short drive from the Swiss border. Its core business was selling mutual funds and, by mainly targeting American servicemen in Europe, it was able to avoid both American and European tax regulations. In 1962, IOS launched its Fund of Funds which was composed entirely of shares in sixteen other mutual funds and management companies. By reinvesting its profits, Cornfeld was able to expand dramatically, acquiring two life-insurance companies with policies of more than $200 million in force, banks in Geneva, Nassau and Luxembourg with combined assets of $12 million, a data-processing firm and other investment services for 80,000 clients from Amsterdam to Ankara.

By now, Cornfeld had 25,000 salesmen who sold his eighteen mutual funds door-to-door to small-time investors throughout Europe. He promised this army of salespeople untold riches and, as a further incentive, would invite them to his palace on Lake Geneva, his Twelfth Century French chateau, his house in London or his Beverly Hills mansion, where they could witness the trappings of the fabulous wealth that could be theirs. Cornfeld also had a permanent suite at a New York hotel, as well as his own fleet of private planes. He is quoted as saying: 'I had mansions all over the world. I threw extravagant parties. And I lived with ten or twelve girls at a time.'

Cornfeld liked to show off his 'harem' of twenty or so beautiful girlfriends who lived in his exotic homes and to display his stables of racehorses and expensive cars. He boasted of his romantic friendships with international glamour girls including Dallas star Victoria Principal, 'Hollywood Madam' Heidi Fleiss, actor George Hamilton's ex-wife Alana Hamilton and Princess Ira of Furstenberg. Cornfeld boasted how his Beverly Hills home was once leased by Douglas Fairbanks and of his friendship with the likes of Victor Lownes, Tony Curtis and Hugh Hefner (whose Playboy Mansion parties Cornfeld regularly visited).

The message to his staff was clear. Few could resist the question he always asked them and for which he became famous: 'Do you sincerely want to be rich?' As far as all the sales people and 100,000 investors in 95 countries were concerned, the answer had to be a resounding 'Yes'.

Around this time, Cornfeld was the subject of a glowing write-up in *Time* magazine. It began: 'Few salesmen leave their jobs just because the boss does not take their advice on company policy, but Bernard Cornfeld is no ordinary salesman. Nine years ago, he told his bosses at Manhattan's Investors Planning Corp, a mutual-fund sales firm, that they ought to expand. The bosses said no; Cornfeld quit. He went overseas himself, set up a company that began by selling mutual-fund shares to GIs and has since become the largest mutual-fund sales organization outside the US. Last week, Cornfeld closed a nostalgic deal to get back into the US mutual-fund field – by buying the company he once quit.' The article went on to describe Cornfeld's lavish lifestyle. 'All this has nicely enriched life for Istanbul-born, Brooklyn-reared Bernie Cornfeld, a mild-mannered bachelor of 37 who does not look as if he would ever talk back to his boss. He drives a Lancia Flaminia Convertible, sails a 42-ft Corsair, owns a ski lodge and a castle in France and lives in a lavish villa in suburban Geneva with two Great Danes and a Chinese houseman. He decorates his penthouse office with red silk

Empire furnishings and swarms of attractive, multilingual secretaries, train and entertain his worldwide force of salesmen with everything from art lectures to cocktails parties in a 50-room lakeside mansion.'

As punters rushed to part with their savings, IOS grew into a mammoth insurance and investment fund which controlled more that £1 billion in stocks and shares. Within five years, the assets of IOS were spread among investments which included oil prospecting, electronics, insurance and goldfields. Some were profitable, some lost money. In ten years, IOS raised in excess of $2.5 billion, bringing Cornfeld a personal fortune of more than $100 million.

Many of the sales force did indeed become wealthy, earning colossal fees in commissions for enrolling more subscribers. But most of the unfortunate investors made little or nothing – and many lost the lot as their funds were squandered to sustain the unashamed luxury of the wild-spending IOS boss. Even the company's investment certificates were flamboyant. Printed by the Canadian Banknote Company, they had ornate borders with a vignette of a semi-nude female sitting in front of a major industrial building with the company's logo on it. They bore the signatures of IOS officers including the president, Cornfeld.

But the bubble had to burst. IOS needed to expand at an impossible rate to keep paying its sales commissions, quite apart from the perks of the boss himself. Indeed, Cornfeld's publicly excessive lifestyle scandalised the conservative Swiss financial authorities and they announced that they were investigating his entire set-up. There were worries that IOS assets were being mismanaged, and that much of its wealth existed only on paper. The market then dropped and the investors' guaranteed dividends had to be paid directly out of the capital. In effect, the operation had become a pyramid scheme. IOS was forced into Initial Public Offering (or public offering of its stock) to meet its costs. The next bear market made many investors cash in their bonds and the IOS stock value decreased further. Cornfeld blamed a 'bear raid' and claimed that a number of German banks had been selling the stock short.

By 1970, nervous investors shared the alarm of international bankers. The share value sank swiftly from its original $18. Many IOS punters could do no more than suffer in silence, for they had broken the currency laws of their own countries by investing in overseas stock. Others refused to take their losses lying down. Cornfeld formed an investment pool with some other investors but they lost when the share value dropped to $2. Even IOS employees and portfolio managers sold their shares. At an angry shareholders' meeting in May 1979, Cornfeld was removed from control of Investors Overseas Services, protesting at his loss of power over the company he had single-handedly created. He was even more upset as his own personal share of the firm dwindled in value to £4 million.

A group of IOS employees complained to the Swiss authorities that Cornfeld and his co-founders pocketed part of the proceeds of a share issue raised among employees in 1969. As a result, he was charged with fraud in 1973 and was arrested when he visited Geneva. He protested his innocence, blaming any fraud on other IOS executives, but he served eleven months in a Swiss jail before being freed on a bail surety of $600,000, when he was told not to leave the country. Cornfeld's trial did not take place until 1979 and lasted three weeks. At the end of it, the judge, Pierre Fournier, finally acquitted him.

While Cornfeld had been languishing in a Swiss cell, unable to control the fortunes of his old company, another American financial entrepreneur had taken over IOS as president. His name was Robert Vesco, the high school dropout son of a Detroit car worker. The fact that the dour, poker-faced Vesco was as far removed from flamboyant Cornfeld as chalk from Swiss cheese encouraged shareholders to trust the newcomer as their financial saviour. They could not have been more wrong.

Vesco, who lived an almost spartan life far removed from the spotlight of publicity that Cornfeld had bathed in, began a ruthless policy of translating the far-flung assets of IOS into hard cash. He managed to salvage some £150 million. The gratitude of the shareholders was short-lived, however, for Robert Vesco vanished – and so did most of the money. Vesco used $500 million worth of IOS money to cover his own investments in his International Controls Corp. Meanwhile, IOS collapsed. American authorities issued a warrant for Vesco's arrest in 1974 but the combined resources of the FBI and the CIA could not catch him as he island-hopped around the Caribbean, increasing his ill-gotten gains by investing in the Bahamas, Costa Rica, Cuba and Panama.

Vesco suffered one dramatic setback when, in May 1974, pilot Alwyn Eisenhauer flew to Panama on behalf of a group of IOS creditors. Eisenhauer marched onto an airfield where Vesco's private Boeing 707 airliner was parked and told the startled ground crew that he was taking his 'boss' on a sudden business trip. Vesco could only watch in anguish from the balcony of his heavily guarded villa near the airfield as his plane roared into the air and vanished in the direction of the United States. The plucky pilot claimed his bounty when the jet was sold by IOS creditors for $10 million!

Meanwhile, Cornfeld, fresh from the confines of a Swiss jail cell, realised that his fair-weather friends had deserted him and began to think seriously about his lifestyle. He developed an obsession for health foods and vitamins, gave up eating red meat and rarely drank alcohol. He also decided for the first time that he wanted a wife and family. In 1976, he married model Loraine Armbruster at his Beverly Hills mansion and the couple went on to have a daughter, Jessica. Nevertheless, despite his best intentions, Cornfeld found it hard to settle, once declaring that polygamy was 'considerably simpler than monogamy and a lot more fun'.

Jail might have been a hiatus in Cornfeld's life but he was still worth around $1.85 million – a nice little nest egg that he had managed to salt away before the final crash of Investors Overseas Services. Although creditors had seized his beloved Beverly Hills estate, he continued to live in style in Europe, always enjoying the finest of wines and surrounding himself with the most beautiful of women. Indeed, after he died of a stroke in London in 1995, his daughter wrote a newspaper article, titled *My Father, the Playboy Who Could Never Get Enough Lovers,* revealing that until his final days he had maintained a close friendship with Heidi Fleiss, who ran

Hollywood's most notorious assembly of high-class hookers. The old rogue had died as he had lived, surrounded by glamour.

While Bernie Cornfeld ended his days happily settled back into his life of luxury, Robert Vesco lived a life constantly on the run. He spent a quarter of a century eluding the authorities as he found refuge in Caribbean and Central American states that lacked extradition treaties with America.

Despite the riches he won from looting IOS, Vesco continued to pursue a criminal career that included drug trafficking, money laundering, making illegal contributions to politicians and plotting to bribe US officials to allow Libya to buy American military aircraft. He even tried to establish his own mini-state in the Caribbean by raising funds on Antigua to buy part of the neighbouring island of Barbuda and form a principality called 'the Sovereign Order of New Aragon'.

After hiding out in Costa Rica under the protection of its president, Jose Figueres Ferrer, and in Nicaragua under the communist Sandinista National Liberation Front, Vesco finally settled in Cuba, where Fidel Castro's government accepted him 'for humanitarian reasons'. For a decade, he lived a life of luxury in Havana, where he kept a lavish estate, a $200 million yacht and a coterie of drinking buddies that included president Castro's brother, Ramon. However, Ramon and Vesco fell out in 1996 when Vesco was jailed for fraud after persuading the Castro family to invest in a supposed wonder-drug that would cure cancer, Aids, arthritis and the common cold.

Freed in 2005, he died at the age of 71 in November 2007. An official confirmation of the old rogue's demise was not issued by the Cuban authorities until May the following year – but only after speculation that he had faked his death to elude the forces of law and order yet again.

CHAPTER 22

Honour at a Price

 policeman described him thus: 'There was an air of
the bogus about him. As soon as I saw him, I said,
"Hello, here's a crook if ever I saw one". He was too
well-dressed, with too much oil on his hair and too
many rings.'

The man so described, Arthur John Peter Michael Maundy
Gregory, was no backstreet chancer, however. His demeanour
may have given him away instantly to a humble English officer
of the law but it failed to ring alarm bells among the great and
powerful in the land – including the Prime Minister at the
time, David Lloyd George.

Through his carefully cultivated connections with the
political hierarchy and the nobility, with leaders of society and
fashion, and with the new captains of industry, Maundy
Gregory was able not only to mix with the titled classes but
literally to create them. For these were the early days of the
Twentieth Century, and 'cash for honours' was as big a
scandal then as it became again a century later. It was a system
which appealed greatly to a snobbish, self-seeking and shallow
stratum of British society: to be instantly elevated to the apex
of aristocracy by a discreet payment for a knighthood or
peerage. And rascally entrepreneur Maundy Gregory was just
the man to fulfill their dreams.

Born in 1877, the son of a Southampton clergyman, Gregory
dropped out of Oxford University to carve himself a career in
the theatre, initially as an actor and later as an impresario.
While portraying fantasy characters for the audience, he also
wove fantastic stories about himself. By the time he was in his
thirties, he had climbed the social ladder by deceit and had
established himself as a 'fixer' in the political world.

His get-rich-quick scheme was simple. It was just after the
end of the First World War and Liberal Prime Minister Lloyd

George was quite blatantly selling peerages and other honours to those who wanted them. This had two benefits: the money received was useful to boost party funds and, of course, recipients of the grand titles were only too happy to pledge their eternal political support in the House of Lords. Gregory realised that this was a 'no questions asked' arrangement and decided to sell titles too.

Oozing confidence and charm, the monocled mercenary inveigled his way into the circles of the wealthy and ambitious. From these people he soon learned who was most likely to earn a mention in the annual Honours Lists of the Monarch and the Prime Minister. Armed with this information, he would then approach those most likely to receive an honour – and offer to 'sell' them what they would have freely received anyway.

Gregory had a different story for each group of his new-found friends. To some, he was a high-ranking member of the Foreign Office; to others he was head of the Secret Service. Above all, they believed Gregory had great influence with people powerful enough to ensure certain names turned up on those all-important Honours Lists. Just in case anyone did express an interest in Gregory's family background, he had a ready-made answer: a 'family tree', four feet long and showing his ancestry right back to Edward III. 'The blood of eight English kings runs through my veins,' he boasted.

His rise to serious power and influence began after the election of 1918 which Lloyd George won, but with a seriously split Liberal Party. This deprived the Premier of a viable party machine of his own, and he desperately need money to fund one. Lloyd George and his Chief Whip, Frederick Guest, cast around for a 'Mr Fixit'. According to one newspaper: 'They needed a gentleman – or someone who gave the appearance of being a gentleman. Somebody who was politically neutral but who could be disowned if things blew up in this face.'

That 'gentleman' was at hand. Completing his facade as a man of impressive social standing, Gregory had already set himself up in luxurious offices not far from the Prime Minister's London residence in Downing Street. He even had his own commissionaire standing guard at his office front door. To impress visitors even more, Gregory organised phone calls to interrupt meetings, and visitors would sit enthralled as Gregory 'advised the Prime Minister' on matters of state. Gregory also used the premises to launch a fiercely patriotic and anti-Communist magazine, *Whitehall Gazette*, to which many of Gregory's visitors, including judges, ambassadors, civil servants and barristers, willingly contributed articles. It all helped elevate his social standing even further.

Often, Gregory found the industrialists and businessmen of the *nouveaux riches* would be so anxious for praiseworthy mention in the *Whitehall Gazette* that they were willing to pay for favourable articles about themselves. Prompted by the discreet suggestions of Lloyd George's right-hand man Frederick Guest, Gregory looked to these rich social climbers to spend their cash on more dramatic elevations to their social standing. With his political masters' approval, he began offering nominated candidates a knighthood for £10,000 or a baronetcy for £40,000. These were fabulous figures for the time, and earned Gregory a commission of about £1,000 a title, netting him a fortune of up to £30,000 a year.

Through flattery and bribery, Gregory soon drew up regular 'Honours Lists' of his own. These comprised not only those in line for an honour anyway but those desperate enough to pay for one. Likely candidates were sent letters suggesting a meeting to discuss a matter of 'great confidentiality'. These almost invariably ended with Gregory's guests parting with anything from £10,000 for a knighthood to £100,000 for a peerage. They were all too greedy to realise that, in many cases, they would have been quite likely to have received their honours anyway.

Gregory's reputation grew. Soon rich businessmen approached him directly with their requests. In most cases, those hopeful of an honour were only too happy to part with their money straight away. On one occasion, however, a cautious businessman wrote Gregory a cheque for £50,000 – but signed it with the title he wanted Gregory to put his way. This of, course, meant that Gregory could only cash the cheque if he fulfilled the deal.

As Gregory's promises of honours became more widespread, so did people's suspicions. Titles were going to the 'wrong people'. In 1921 honours went to shipbuilder Rowland Hodge, a convicted wartime food hoarder, and to Sir William Vestey, a tax dodger. The following year, convicted fraudster Sir Joseph Robinson paid £30,000 for a peerage. The tycoon was forced to decline it, however, after King George V described the peerage as 'little less than an insult to the Crown'.

Gregory's business took a further knock when Lloyd George's government fell to the Conservatives under Stanley Baldwin, who in 1925 passed legislation outlawing the trading of honours. It was not enough to deter the arrogant Gregory, so in 1927 the Conservative Party called in Scotland Yard's Special Branch to launch an undercover operation against him. Police infiltrated Gregory's organisation and obtained a list of people who had paid for honours – and made sure they never got them.

The conman's trade in honours dried up and he was reduced to selling dubious foreign and even Papal titles. He ran a Mayfair club, which continued to give him access to the rich and famous – but he no longer had anything further than expensive cocktails to sell to them. He next took a lease on a hotel in Surrey, which became known by its wealthy patrons as an establishment where young ladies could be entertained with no questions asked. At this time, Gregory, though himself preferring the romantic company of men, was squiring a musical actress named Edith Rosse, whom he often introduced as his wife.

Maundy Gregory's standing finally collapsed in 1932 when he was sued by the executors of a businessman who had paid him £30,000 for a baronetcy he had never received. Bankruptcy loomed but Gregory was saved from penury – and survived another scandal – following the sudden death of Mrs Rosse, who recently had suspiciously changed her will in his favour. It was accepted as legal, even though it was penned in Gregory's handwriting on the menu of a London restaurant.

There were now whispers that Maundy Gregory was not just a Machiavellian master manipulator of political favours but a murderer. A double murderer, in fact, because of the mysterious disappearance of one of his political opponents a decade earlier.

A former Socialist MP, Victor Grayson, had launched a campaign to clean up the 'cash for honours' system instituted by Lloyd George immediately after the First World War. In one widely reported speech, he said: 'The sale of honours is a national scandal. It can be traced right down to Number 10 Downing Street, and to a monocled dandy with offices in Whitehall. I know this man and one day I will name him.' Grayson was beaten up by thugs in The Strand, London, in September 1920 but refused to be silenced. Two weeks later, he was dining with friends when he took a phone call and hurried off to a 'brief meeting in a hotel in Leicester Square'. He was never seen again.

The subsequent demise of Mrs Rosse, and the hastily scribbled will leaving her £18,000 estate to Gregory, again raised suspicions that the conman was also a killer. Her doctor diagnosed 'poisoning' as cause of death but no tests were made on her body, which Gregory arranged to be buried in an open coffin in boggy ground.

Gregory may have got away with murder but, ultimately, he failed to escape justice entirely. In 1933 he was prosecuted under the Honours (Prevention and Abuses) Act. One charge was that of attempting to obtain £10,000 from a Lieutenant Commander E.W.B. Leake DSO, a notable figure in sporting and social circles, who had reported Gregory's false offer of a title. Gregory at first denied all charges against him. He then changed his plea to guilty – a move that had much of British society sighing with relief, for such a plea meant there would be no long drawn-out court case, no names and no scandal. Gregory, still the only person to be jailed under the Honours Act, was sentenced to two months in prison and fined £50. He served his time at London's Wormwood Scrubs prison.

On his release, he went into 'exile' in Paris where he lived comfortably on the income from the estate of poor Mrs Rosse – and, it is believed, a pension secretly paid by the government to keep his silence over exactly who had sought and received honours.

By now a drink-sodden old man, Maundy Gregory's final demise was ignominious. When the Second World War broke out, he was living in the seaside resort of Dieppe. Captured and imprisoned, he died of a heart attack brought on in a military hospital near Paris in August 1941. Buried in a local cemetery, his bones were later disinterred and dumped in a charnel house.

CHAPTER 23

All that Glitters

T here is something about diamonds and gold that never fails to lure fortune-hunters – or tricksters trying to capitalise on the desire for such treasures. History is full of such frauds. So it is no wonder that one scam, called the 'gold brick', became an epithet applied to anyone who would rather cheat and steal than earn an honest crust – a term of abuse that remains in use today.

Quite simply, the 'gold brick' trick involved selling a 'gold bar' that was really gold-coated lead. In the 1850s, a gold brick was just that: a brick-shaped block of gold that had been cast at a mine for easy transport. One report in *Harper's New Monthly Magazine* in 1888, described a gold brick cast in Montana as being 'a trifle larger than the common clay brick' but weighing nearly 32 pounds (roughly 14.5kg). However, as a result of what the press at the time called 'the celebrated gold brick swindle', the term took on a different meaning.

It was in October 1879, that Mr N. D. Clark, the president of the First National Bank of Ravenna, Ohio, visited a mine he owned at Leadville in Colorado. There he was approached by five miners, who asked him to advance money on a 52-pound gold brick which for some reason they weren't able to ship at the time. The owner told a hard-luck story about having lost all his property and urgently needing money. Mr Clark had the brick taken to a blacksmith, who cut off one corner and pronounced the gold to be genuine. Upon this declaration, Mr Clark advanced the miner $10,000 on condition that the brick, and the miner, accompanied him to Chicago to get the balance. The miner, of course, vanished off the train on the way, and Mr Clark found to his chagrin that the gold brick was not all it seemed. The corners were gold right enough but the body of the brick was worthless.

This wasn't the first attempt at this style of fraud, of course, and a number of copycat attempts at selling people fake gold bricks followed. The phrase 'to sell someone a gold brick' entered the language meaning to swindle someone, and 'to gold brick' came to mean perpetrating a fraud. At some point in time, the term also came to refer to a criminal who would do anything, including sell fake gold bricks, rather than do an honest day's work.

When it comes to gold, greedy fools are certainly the best targets. They are the greatest gifts to the confidence trickster. In 1897, American Baptist priest Prescott Ford Jernegan dazzled investors with his 'gold accumulator'. When lowered into the ocean, the contraption sucked particles of the precious metal out of the surrounding waters. Hours later when it was lifted above the waves, it was coated in solid gold. Jernegan announced: 'You see, there is a huge amount of tiny gold flakes swirling about in the oceans, particularly near the Maine shoreline. All you need to collect the gold is a special machine.' Knowing a good thing when they saw it, investors shelled out $300,000 to buy stock in his new company. Unfortunately the success of the device had more to do with the diving skills of Jernegan's accomplice, Charles E. Fisher, than it did with any accumulative powers the machine might have had. Jernegan managed to flee to France with over $100,000 before the scam was discovered.

Alchemists, those mediaeval chemists who believed they had the Midas touch, tried desperately to turn common metals into gold – and even the realisation that this could not be achieved did not prevent them from taking money from those who still believed it could.

Tricks of the alchemist's trade were reported in a paper, read in 1722, at the Royal Academy of Science in Paris. It described, for instance, how fraudsters would use a double-bottomed crucible. The upper surface was of wax painted to resemble the lower surface, which was of iron and copper. Between these surfaces, the alchemist would put gold or silver dust. When the pot was heated, a lump of 'gold' would magically appear.

In the early Eighteenth Century, Frenchman Jean Delisle claimed to be able to 'turn lead into gold and iron into silver by merely heating these metals red-hot and pouring upon them in that state some oil and powder he is possessed of, so that it would not be impossible for any man to make a million a day if he had sufficient of this wondrous mixture'. Delisle was invited to Paris by Louis XIV to prove his gold-making technique. Knowing he would be exposed as a fraud, Delisle kept making excuses. Eventually he was arrested in 1711 and taken to the Bastille. He was told to make gold or he would spend the rest of his days in jail. Failing health led to his death in a Bastille dungeon.

The French king's successors, Louis XV and Louis XVI, were also infatuated with the search for a magic formula for precious metals. They fell victim to one of the most notorious alchemy hoaxers of all time, the mysterious Count Saint-Germain. Graceful, charming, dressed like a dandy, his pockets full of glittering diamonds, he persuaded the royals and other rich patrons to fund a string of laboratories where he promised to turn base metals into gold. From 1743, when Louis XV first summoned him to the Palace of Versailles, until the 1770s, when he was exposed as a fraud, Count Saint-Germain travelled Europe producing a myriad coloured paints and dyes but no gold.

Alchemy was an art that reached its pinnacle of plausibility in the Eighteenth Century yet it was still being practised in the early Twentieth Century. One of its arch exponents was Hans Unruh, a cheat who preyed on the rich and aristocratic. This was his sales patter to them: 'I must ask you to treat what I am about to tell you with the strictest confidence. This is not a secret to be shared but one we must keep strictly to ourselves. It is very important. And it could be dangerous.'

Thus Hans Unruh addressed an audience of aristocrats assembled in a Munich hotel suite. As they listened intently to him, they began to believe that they were recipients of the most golden of opportunities ever likely to come their way. As long as they told no one else the amazing secrets he was imparting to them, they were destined to become incredibly wealthy.

All eyes were now unblinkingly on the stranger who had invited them to witness his magical demonstration. Herr

Unruh picked up a salt cellar from the table in front of him and brandished it before the captivated audience. From the contents of this little salt cellar, explained Unruh, would come what everyone in the whole world lusted after: pure gold.

Some guests coughed awkwardly. One stifled a laugh. Unruh waited until he once more had everyone's attention then continued. He was a scientist, he told them, and he had discovered how gold was made. It came from the depths of the earth where it was created by a chemical action on ordinary salt. If some method could be discovered to reproduce this chemical change artificially, unlimited quantities of gold could be manufactured worldwide. And anyone with the knowledge would be very wealthy indeed.

'And I am the man with that knowledge,' said Unruh. 'Please realise how privileged you all are that I choose to share it with you.' Their host paused to allow his words to take effect. Some amongst the gathering wondered whether they were listening to some fool wasting their time yet dared not speak out for fear they might miss a money-making miracle. Others simply sat in silent disbelief. Whatever their private thoughts, the audience were by now becoming more interested in what Unruh had to say.

They once more found it hard not to laugh out loud, however, when Unruh picked up a lamp stand and held it high with a dramatic flourish. He told them research had proved that if you treated salt with a special form of light it would turn into pure gold. Now came Unruh's practical demonstration. He took hold of the salt cellar and gently tapped some of its contents onto a steel plate. Then he took the lamp stand and held it in such a way that the shade completely covered the salt.

He switched on the lamp and waited a few moments. When he finally removed the shade, the onlookers were speechless. There on the plate where grains of salt had once been were bright, glittering flecks of gold dust. To emphasise the value of the little pile, now the object of several pairs of money-hungry eyes, Unruh scooped it up and tipped it into a small pouch.

By now, any disbelief the aristocrats had been harbouring turned to pure greed. Unruh had his guests under his spell.

This was the moment to explain that he was in fact a struggling scientist. If those present wanted to exploit his miraculous discovery, they would have to initially be his financial backers. A great deal of money was need to provide the vital equipment for this very special kind of gold-prospecting.

'You are wealthy, of proven integrity and have a great sense of responsibility,' Unruh told them. 'You have all been specially selected for this opportunity. I wish you all to become shareholders in my enterprise. Perhaps you would like to go away and think it over.' But the guests did not need any more time to consider what all this meant. They wanted to be part of Unruh's gold-making project right now. Thousands of pounds were handed over to Unruh that night. The rich departed happy in the knowledge they would become even richer – and Unruh left knowing he had just pulled off an extremely clever con-trick.

Had his greedy spectators bothered to check the gold before them more closely, they would have realised things were not as they seemed. There was no gold at all, just fine scrapings of brass, but in the right light it looked just like the real thing. Unruh had simply concealed a trickle of this fake 'gold dust' in the lampshade, and when he tapped the shade the 'gold' showered down upon the salt.

Phoney gold and silver 'discoveries' were common in the years following the California Gold Rush of 1849. Tricksters fooled many innocents by 'salting' worthless mines with particles of gold dust. That didn't stop the fortune-hunters from flooding in. From grubby prospectors washing dirt in a thousand Western streams to bankers and speculators in San Francisco, New York and London, everyone, it seemed, wanted to believe that the West's waterbeds and mountains held untold riches.

One report in the *Tucson Weekly Arizonian* in April 1870 referred to a new mine dubbed 'the Mountains of Silver', stating: 'We have found it! The greatest treasures ever discovered on the continent, and doubtless the greatest treasures ever witnessed by the eyes of man.' And so the stage was set for the Great Diamond Hoax, a brilliantly acted scam by two Kentucky cousins that involved some of California's biggest bankers and businessmen, a former commander of the Union Army, a U.S. representative, leading lawyers on both coasts, and the founder of Tiffany & Co.

On a summer day in 1872, two old-timer gold prospectors sauntered into the Bank of California in San Francisco. They were Philip Arnold and John Slack, and the two grizzled old fraudsters were about to pull off one of the cleverest confidence tricks of all time.

Philip Arnold was a poorly-educated former hatter's apprentice, Mexican War veteran and Gold Rush 'Forty-Niner', who had spent twenty years working in mining operations in the West, making enough money to pay for visits back to Kentucky, where he bought a farm, got married and had a family. In 1870, he was working as an assistant book-keeper for the Diamond Drill Company, a San Francisco drill maker that used diamond-headed bits. For a bookkeeper, Arnold, then just past forty, showed a surprising interest in the industrial-grade diamonds that kept the drills running. He even read up on the subject.

By November that year, Arnold had acquired a bag of uncut diamonds which he mixed with garnets, rubies and sapphires that he had probably bought from Indians in Arizona. By now, he also had a partner, John Slack, an older cousin from Kentucky who, like Arnold, had fought in the Mexican War and had gone after gold in 1849.

As they walked through the doors of the Bank of California, Arnold and Slack had every reason to feel happy with life for, as a greedy bank teller was to discover, they were bearing a wonderful hoard. The two men slammed a drawstring sack on the counter and demanded that it be kept in the bank's safe then, satisfied that their 'deposit' was in safe-keeping, the two old prospectors wandered off to find a saloon in which to celebrate their good fortune. Watching all this was a teller with a strong feeling that here was a chance to cash in.

As soon as Arnold and Slack were out of sight, the teller peeked into the sack. He was expecting to see a handful or two of gold. Instead his eyes focused on more stunning, sparkling uncut diamonds than he had ever seen before in his life. The startled teller picked the bag up and ran into the office of bank boss William Ralston, who had become wealthy through dubious deals but was always on the lookout for fresh ways of increasing his fortune. After examining the diamonds, he now had visions of becoming America's Diamond King.

Promising the teller a suitable reward for his troubles, Ralston told him to seek out the two prospectors straight away. Ralston himself joined in the search. It took three anxious days before the prospectors were tracked down. Arnold and Slack were extremely drunk and wanted only to drink some more. They could not understand what Ralston wanted with them. Ralston could not understand what they were saying and had to stay with them, patiently waiting for them to sober up.

After much coaxing, and with Ralston's promise of financial backing, Arnold and Slack eventually told the bank chief that they had found a diamond field 'bigger than Kimberley'. But they had not acquired title to the land yet and so refused to tell him exactly where it was. They would however, allow anyone who wanted to see the diamond field to do so – as long as their visitor made the entire journey blindfolded. Ralston, his imagination swimming with diamonds in unbelievable quantities, agreed. He didn't fancy making the journey himself, however, and instead sent mining engineer David Calton who returned and thrust diamonds under Ralston's nose. A deal was struck. Assuming he was dealing with unsophisticated country bumpkins, Ralston already had it in his mind to take control of the diamond mine.

Ralston paid Arnold and Slack $50,000, put another $300,000 aside for any expenses incurred, and pledged them a further $350,000 when they started producing their promised harvest of diamonds. By now, word had spread about the diamond prospectors' land. Everyone wanted to be part of the scheme. Joining forces with a number of other prominent San Francisco financiers, Ralston formed the New York Mining and Commercial Company, capitalised at $10 million, and began selling stock to eager investors. Convinced that the American West must have many other major deposits of diamonds, at least 25 other diamond exploration companies formed in the subsequent months. Those who contributed money included Baronet Anthony de Rothschild, the editor Horace Greeley, General George B. McClellan and Charles Lewis Tiffany, founder of the world's largest jewellery business.

To ensure that there was nothing untoward about what David Colton had claimed to have seen, Ralston sent along a group of witnesses to Arnold and Slack's gold field. The group included well-respected mining engineer, Henry Janin selected by the San Francisco investors.

Cold weather meant Janin could not visit the fields until June. Arnold and Slack met up with him and a group of other Ralston representatives. The group boarded a Union Pacific train to Rawlins, Wyoming. Though the spot that Arnold had picked to salt was closer to the Black Buttes, Wyoming, station, the two tricksters wanted to keep the exact location secret, so led the blindfolded party on a confusing four-day horseback journey, often pretending to be lost and climbing hills to get his bearings. When their blindfolds were removed, the visitors felt they were dreaming. Ant hills in the valley shimmered and sparkled with diamond dust. Not only that, diamonds as big as a man's thumb and other gems were scattered across the earth. In retrospect, what the group found was laughable. One commented later: 'He held up something glittering in his hand. For more than an hour, diamonds were being found in profusion, together with occasional rubies, emeralds and sapphires. Why a few pearls weren't thrown in for good luck I have never yet been able to tell. Probably it was an oversight.'

It was when the party reported their findings back to Ralston that he decided to get rid of Arnold and Slack and have every gem for himself. He threatened the two prospectors with legal claims, saying they had no rights. He bullied them into backing down from the deal they had made with him. Apparently worn down by Ralston's harassment, Arnold and Slack agreed to accept $700,000 for their share of the diamond field. They were then told to leave town.

News of the diamond 'Klondike' soon spread around the world. But what finally led to the hoax's collapse was an encounter on an Oakland-bound train between Janin and members of a government survey team led by Clarence King, a Yale-educated geologist. King had come West in 1863 at the age of 21, travelling by wagon train with a friend and joining the California Geological Survey. By the early 1870s, he and the three dozen men under his command had surveyed, mapped and described the whole immense patch of the West within their domain, and the fieldwork for what was known as the Fortieth Parallel Survey was nearly done.

King and his team were obviously aware of the supposed diamond harvests but most of the rumoured discoveries had been in Arizona and New Mexico, outside the survey's boundaries. So it was alarming for the team to hear from Janin that a major discovery of diamonds had been found on their 'patch' – a discovery that would make them out to be less than thorough in their surveys. King and his men decided that they had better inspect the diamond fields as soon as possible. In October 1872, King and his team travelled east by train from Oakland to Fort Bridger, Wyoming, where mules took them on the final leg of their journey.

Arriving at the supposed diamond site, King and his team began to inspect the unusual field. King uncovered a stone partially polished and definitely not natural. He noticed the field had diamonds, rubies, emeralds and sapphires in the same area and many of the gems were in places they could not have reached by any natural means; in fact, the stones were only found in ground that had quite obviously been disturbed, rubies being discovered in anthills that were surrounded by footprints. The team's report was later to state: 'Our explanation was that someone must have pushed in a ruby or two on the end of a stick.'

It was later to be revealed that Arnold and Slack had bought a bundle of cheap cast-off diamonds – refuse left over from gem cutting in London and Amsterdam – and scattered them to 'salt' the ground. Most of the gems were originally from South Africa.

When word of the hoax came out, Ralston was a laughing stock. And when the painstaking nature of the amazing con-trick perpetrated by Arnold and Slack came to light, they became popular heroes. This is how they had done it. The pair had gone to Europe and spent their life savings of $35,000 on buying hoards of fake gems. They had increased the number of gems even more by using a lapidary tool to split each 'diamond' into pieces. Then they had spread them around the carefully chosen site.

Public sympathy was very much on the side of the colluding cousins, who even managed to escape prosecution. The *San Francisco Chronicle* described the duo's scam as: 'The most gigantic and barefaced swindle of the age, the scheme being noteworthy for the manner of its unraveling and its colorful characters. Not only did it propel to prominence a geologist later befriended and admired by Theodore Roosevelt, it also gave a fed-up American public some hope that honest science could triumph, at least occasionally, over hucksterism and greed.'

Ralston returned $80,000 to each of his investors, but of course was never able to recover the $600,000 given to the perpetrators of the Great Diamond Hoax. Arnold returned to his home in Elizabethtown, Kentucky, where he founded his own bank and lived out the few remaining years of his life in luxury. He died of pneumonia in 1878 after he was wounded in a shoot-out with a rival banker. Slack apparently went to St Louis, where he owned a coffin-making company. He later moved to White Oaks, New Mexico, where he carried on his trade and lived a quiet life until (making use of one of his own caskets) he died in 1896.

Ralston ended up ruined, his financial empire collapsed and his dreams of owning his very own diamond field shattered.

CHAPTER 24

Tycoon of Cell 10 B3

As it says in the Florida Administrative Code for Prisons: 'Each inmate shall be provided with reasonable access to a telephone at reasonable times.' The battered black telephone provided by Florida's prison service for the use of their prisoners was the key to Daniel Faries' nefarious trade. It was all he needed to let his fingers do the stealing – the only tool he needed to pull off one of the most fantastic, yet little known, frauds in history.

Faries spent most of his adult life as guest of the US Government in various Houses of Correction, where not much seems to have been done to correct him. He was a petty thief and, judging by the number of times he was caught, not even a very clever one. But what the one craft he found he really was good at was conning. His prolonged periods of incarceration turned out to be the most lucrative years of his life as the failed small-time crook proved himself to be an inspirational entrepreneur, running a multi-million dollar business from within prison. His cells may have had cheap furniture, curtainless windows and bare walls but they became his 'executive offices' where, under the eyes of the guards, he made a fortune from fraud. And it was all done on the telephone.

Danny Faries' main problem was that when he wasn't behind bars, he was leaning on them getting drunk. And when he wasn't drunk, he was drying out. In March 1986, he was halfway through a course of treatment at a clinic in Jacksonville, Florida, when he decided to go back on the booze in a big way. A pal of his was having a party down south in the fleshpots of Miami, so Faries broke out of the clinic, stole a van and hightailed it to where the action was. It was some party. After two days' solid drinking, the shindig degenerated into arguments and brawls. Faries said later that someone handed him a gun and, although he couldn't recall why, he shot his old pal three times in the head. Surprisingly, his pal survived but when police raided the house and found the trappings of drug-taking, the injured man was questioned and taken to hospital. The following evening, police were again called to the house where they found Faries in the backyard, unconscious and reeking of booze, with the gun in the waistband of his trousers. He readily confessed to the shooting – and unfortunately, when his buddy died in hospital two months later, found himself charged with first-degree murder

For the next four years, Faries was locked up in Dade County Jail awaiting trial. There, he shared a dormitory-style cell with up to 30 fellow inmates and, because they were all on remand, they had access to a telephone in the cell. That one shared telephone was theirs of right, a privilege enshrined in Florida Administrative Code for Prisons, section 33–8.009(9). This phone must have been one of the most used in the whole of the state, as Faries sat beside it night and day, skilfully employing it to defraud total strangers. With other people's credit card details, he ordered goods and services for accomplices on the outside, for his fellow jailbirds, for himself, even for his prison guards. His business, which became known among Miami villains as the 'Jailhouse Shopping Network', boomed to the tune of $3 million.

How it worked was amazingly ingenious but, at the same time, frighteningly simple. First, Faries would phone his pals and tell them to go 'Dumpster Diving': underworld slang for rummaging around in skips and rubbish bins looking for the discarded credit card slips that were so common at the time. Faries knew how careless people could be with their carbon receipts, receipts that contained the name and number of the cardholder. Armed with the numbers from his 'divers', Faries would then phone the credit card companies pretending to be a retailer checking on a sale. Thinking it was a genuine inquiry, they would give him the address and the credit limit of the cardholder.

Faries would then call, say, an electrical store and order their most expensive hi-fi, paying over the phone with the credit card details he had just been given. In case the firm checked, he would ask that the hi-fi be delivered to the cardholder's real address at a particular time. Faries would then call his 'diver' with details of the purchase, the time it was to be delivered and the name and address of the cardholder. At the appointed hour, the 'diver' would hang around outside the address. When the delivery van drew up, he would saunter over and say: 'Hey. I'm Mr So-and-so. That's my new hi-fi you've got there. Thanks a lot.' He would sign for the package, wait till the van had driven off, then head straight for the city where any one of a thousand 'fences' would give him hard cash for the goods.

The downside was that thousands of shocked credit card holders would look at their statements every month and discover they had bought a new TV, a slap-up meal at a top restaurant, an airline ticket to South America or a new Armani suit, courtesy of Danny Faries and his amazing jailhouse shopping fraud. But the scam worked like a dream and, from his 'office' in cell 10 B 3 of Dade County Jail, the failed thief was becoming, on paper at least, a very rich man.

Sometimes, if he wasn't sure of an address, he would have goods delivered to the jail itself. The stores and card companies never checked, although the delivery drivers and prison guards must have raised an eyebrow at the high-class merchandise passing through the prison gates. Faries and his fellow inmates soon became the best dressed convicts in America, wearing designer jogging suits and flash jewellery. 'Oh, yes sir, I had a bumper business,' Faries told a jail visitor. 'It's so easy to find confederates. I never took more than half. I split half with everybody. I got robbed a lot but you just take it on the chin. Heck, it's all free.'

Even when credit card companies began to abandon the idea of carbon receipts, Faries had an answer. He formed a network of crooked sales assistants at shops, bars and restaurants and paid them $20 a piece for every card number they gave him. He would get his team to ask the cardholders to jot down their addresses and phone numbers so they could 'check the card's authenticity'. Grateful cardholders were happy to oblige, impressed at such security measures which prevented their precious cards falling into the wrong hands. Little did they know that the information they were providing would be relayed by phone to a cell block in Dade County Jail.

Faries was beginning to look upon himself as a Robin Hood character. He reasoned that the smart cardholder, after the initial shock of seeing his outrageous statement at the end of the month, would promptly contact the authorities and have the offending item struck from his bill. It would be the profit-bloated card companies who would ultimately pick up the tab. His Jailhouse Shopping Network even branched out into the world of philanthropy. He used the stolen credit card numbers to pledge thousands of dollars to charity: starving children, the homeless, the sick and the aged. All from the phone in cell 10 B 3.

More in his own interests, Faries also ordered up presents for his cellmates and their relatives. If a fellow inmate was unable to celebrate his wedding anniversary because he was locked up, Faries would make sure that his wife got a bunch of roses and a gift of jewellery, bought with some poor unsuspecting victim's credit card.

Faries subsequently claimed that his guards also got their fair share of his ill-gotten largesse. 'All the correctional officers knew what I was doing,' he told a reporter when the story of his prison business reached the Florida newspapers. 'Their families knew what I was doing because they were receiving gifts on every holiday, birthday and anniversary.' Faries told a CBS television newsman: 'The officers are just working stiffs, they're not making much money, and they're seeing all this stuff going on. They're hearing about Dom Perignon champagne and trips to the Caribbean. So I try to send things at Christmas and on holidays.' The interviewer then asked Faries what it cost the guards. He replied: 'Oh no! Perish the thought. No sir!'

Prison officials denied accusations about gifts from Faries but there was no secret made of his generosity towards charities. His explanation was that, with nothing to do in his cell but watch television, he would see reports of famine and hunger and would immediately get on the phone to pledge a credit card donation. He reckoned that if the victims of his frauds had actually seen the television pictures of famine victims, they'd have made the donation themselves.

The first hiccup in this otherwise smooth operation came in September 1987 when Faries, ever generous with other people's money, decided to hold a party for a group of fellow inmates who were all being released at the same time. Using the credit card number of a certain unsuspecting Dr Felix Entwhistle, he booked a suite at the luxurious Mayfair House Hotel in downtown Miami. From his cell, the unselfish Faries ordered the best champagne and wall-to-wall call-girls for his newly freed chums. And all night they toasted Dr Entwhistle whose gold card was making the evening possible.

By midnight, however, a member of the hotel staff, concerned at the quality of the guests, who hardly looked like a convention of eminent physicians, decided to check on Dr. Entwhistle's credit limit. It amounted to $2,500, which by then had been well and truly spent. The hotel employee found a sober member of the raucous party and suggested that credit had run out. A phone call was made and within minutes an indignant 'Dr Entwhistle' was on the telephone to the hotel's night manager, furious at the treatment of his guests. The credit limit was immediately extended, and the manager apologised for spoiling the doctor's party.

Some weeks later, the real Dr Entwhistle was equally indignant when he got on the phone to his credit card company. Following his complaint, Detective Raul Ubieta of the Metro-Dade Police visited the Mayfair House to discover that no one, genuinely, could remember who had signed the bill as the party wound up. There was, however, a hotel record of a phone call made from the suite that night. It was a local number: 5454494. Detective Ubieta dialled the number – and got Dade County Jail cell 10 B 3. The game appeared to be up for Faries.

A special Metro-Dade police investigation unit, headed by Ubieta and fellow officer Lieutenant Ross, moved in on the Jailhouse Shopping Network. They bugged the phone in Faries' cell and recorded all numbers dialled. Ubieta was stunned by the result. 'We'd never seen anything like this', he said. 'He was making orders all over the place for everybody – airline tickets, video equipment, computers, clothes. The hours he worked were outrageous.' Sometimes police noticed a sharp decrease in the number of calls. They were worried that Faries might have smelled a rat. But an informant would tell them that the 'Managing Director' of the Jailhouse Shopping Network was high on drugs: Faries had simply taken a day off.

One of the tactics of Ubieta and his team was to try to intercept the goods Faries had just ordered over the phone. 'I'd call the suppliers and point out to them they had just been the victims of a fraud,' said Ubieta. 'Many of them got angry and said that the card was genuine and that they had checked the address and phone number. They were furious that they were losing trade. I never mentioned to them that the number belonged to Dade County Jail. They would never have believed me.'

Evidence against Faries and his accomplices was accumulating satisfactorily when, suddenly, a major part of the police case collapsed. The Dade County Department of Corrections, who understandably had not been informed of the police investigation since some of their officers were on uncomfortably close terms with Faries, organised a search of cell 10 B 3. They found 300 stolen credit card numbers, with names, addresses, phone numbers and credit limits, requests for merchandise and even the scribbled text of messages to go with flowers ordered over the phone. Police were furious at the cell shakedown. They had hoped to gain enough evidence to nail not only Faries but also his associates working on the outside and, hopefully, any prison officers who might be on the take from the inside. As it was, they had to cut their losses, believing that at least they had enough evidence to get a conviction against Faries himself.

After the cell raid, the detectives confronted Faries. 'He was no problem,' an officer recalled. 'He showed us how he did everything. He told us he'd order up lobster dinners for the guards and how they allowed him to get laid during visits.' Metro-Dade Police handed over all their statements and evidence to the Florida State Attorney's office and waited for fraud charges to be brought. But nothing happened. At first, they were told that charges would have to wait pending the outcome of Faries' murder trial. Then, months later, the case against the Jailhouse Shopping Network was suddenly dropped. No official reason was given, although a State Attorney's Office official was reported as saying: 'There is very little deterrent value in bringing a couple of minor felonies to court when a guy is facing the electric chair.' In 1989, to the annoyance of the police, the Attorney's Office closed the case once and for all; it added that using the evidence of an accused murderer against prison guards could not lead to a successful prosecution.

Meanwhile, Danny Faries was moved from cell 10 B 3 to cell 104 in the nearby Interim Central Detention Centre. Incredibly, he was still given access to a phone. On hearing this, shocked police investigators demanded a meeting with the Department of Corrections, only to be told that there was 'no legal basis for imposing prohibitions or restrictions on inmates' access to a telephone'. Faries was still in business. In fact, he was delighted with his new office. He had cell 104 to himself and shared the phone with only five other inmates in other cells. He said later: 'About the only difference the move made was to give me some more privacy. I didn't have so many people looking over my shoulder all the time.'

Faries' only problem was that his stock of credit card numbers had dried up, seized from his cell by prison authorities. So, as he later revealed in an interview shown in 1991 on the TV show *Sixty Minutes*, he came up with a new corporate strategy. 'After the raid I still had one hidden card number, written on the bottom of my bunk. It was a woman's card. Regina Donovan was the name. It was a good number and I said, well here we go – we gotta do something!' So he took out an advertisement in the national newspaper *USA Today*, calling himself Regina Donovan Cosmetics. It advertised $90 worth of top-quality women's cosmetics for the bargain price of $19.95, all credit cards accepted. Faries hired an answering service in New York for a week and the calls flooded in. There were no cosmetics, of course, but the callers dutifully left their names, addresses, card numbers, expiry dates.

That was all the information that Faries needed to start up in business again. As he explained: 'The girls took the orders, saying "Thank you for calling Regina Donovan, may we help you and what credit card will we be using today?" They wrote down the number and the expiry date, and at the end of the day I'd call them and they'd have this whole new stack of numbers. It was like a goldmine.' Business boomed and, in a fit of generosity, Faries even ordered an expensive set of weights and work-out equipment for the detention centre gym – on a stolen credit card number, of course.

So how did Faries manage to operate his bizarre one-man crime wave for so long? Asked this question, the man in charge, Director of Dade County Corrections Lonnie Lawrence, commented: 'We don't have a perfect system.' But for Daniel Faries himself, the system was absolutely perfect. As he said: 'If they put you in a room the size of a bathroom for years at a time with only a telephone, you come up with some pretty inventive stuff, because everything you do, you do through the phone. I feel like I constructed a train, and just darn near anybody can drive a train. You don't have to be terribly intelligent and only marginally capable. Heck, it's on a track. All you have to do is put in the fuel – credit card numbers – and this train will go! What I did was not really so smart. And there was certainly nothing very secret about it. It was all pretty wide open. On the outside of my cell door I had Master Card and Visa logos.'

Pete Collins is the man who, at the time, knew more about Danny Faries than perhaps anyone else. A teacher at Jackson High School who became fascinated by the Faries case, he met Faries and began collating material for a book on the amiable conman. In 1991 the row over lack of action taken to curb Faries' excesses became the subject of an investigation in the *Miami Herald*, principally due to the thorough researches of Collins, by now a freelance writer based in Miami.

As Collins told a TV audience: 'When I was interviewing him, you could call him up at any time of the day or night and he would be working around the clock. He was operating in as many as 40 states. There were as many as 150 drop sites, dozens of employees, $750,000 documented in stolen goods – perhaps in reality up to two to four million dollars – and that was just during an eleven-month window of his captivity.'

By early 1989 Faries had managed to postpone his murder trial date several times simply by firing one defence lawyer after another. Around this time, however, a telephone company called TELCO noticed that the number of long-distance calls made on fraudulent credit card numbers had increased in Southern Florida by a staggering 4,000 per cent. Painstakingly, the company went through the figures and was surprised to discover that no fewer than 1,500 of these calls could be traced to the telephone outside Cell 104 of the Interim Central Detention Centre in Dade County. TELCO bypassed both the police and the Corrections Department and called in the US Secret Service. Danny Faries' Jailhouse Shopping Network was about to go into liquidation.

It took ten months for federal agents to get the evidence on Faries. During that time, they established documentary proof that he had stolen $750,000. But they were convinced that the real figure was nearer $4 million. They raided his cell twice and found thousands of credit card numbers. One senior agent asked the Department of Corrections why, in the light of the previous police investigation, the fraudster was still allowed near a phone. He was told that there was an administrative rule that 'this particular class of prisoner in this particular cell block was entitled to access to a telephone'. Rules were made not to be broken.

Faries was locked in his cell 24 hours a day while the Secret Service prepared a case against him. During that time, he was allowed to use the phone for only fifteen minutes, and then under the strictest supervision. But Faries claimed that business went on as usual. He boasted that he managed to run a telephone wire into his cell from the nursing office next door. Someone smuggled him in a telephone and he rigged the whole thing up to his cell light so that, instead of ringing, the light flashed and the guards were not alerted.

But even Danny Faries could postpone his murder trial no longer. On May 16, four years after the original incident, he was convicted of the first-degree murder of his partying pal and was sentenced to 25 years. Federal agents hauled him off to the Metropolitan Correctional Centre in Chicago to await trial on fraud charges. Refusing a defence lawyer and choosing to represent himself in court, he pleaded guilty to one charge of fraud and was given a further five years' jail. Faced with serving his time in a federal prison, Faries suddenly complained of paranoiac visions and went conveniently cuckoo. He was promptly dispatched to Charlotte Correctional Institution near peaceful Fort Myers, on Florida's Gulf Coast, where, in the much higher-security state 'psychiatric facility', he claimed to have put the credit card business behind him.

Cynics were not so sure. They quote the interview with Faries on the *Sixty Minutes* show when host Mike Wallace asked him: 'So what you're saying is you're going straight now at Charlotte Correctional Center?'

Faries replied: 'Yeah – or having to go on a new direction, because the...' Then he thought for a moment and added enigmatically: 'Oh, well, I mean, come on. I'm not just going to roll over, Mr Wallace!'

CHAPTER 25

Lady with the Secret Smile

The *Mona Lisa* is the most famous painting in the history of art and, although more than 500 years old, the lady with the half-smile continues to inspire fascination, reproduction, parody, scientific theory and fierce debate to this day. Painted in oil on a panel of poplar wood by Leonardo da Vinci around 1505, the portrait hangs in the Louvre in Paris. The proper title is '*Portrait of Lisa Gherardini, wife of Francesco del Giocondo*', but in France she is known as *La Joconde*, in Italy *La Gioconda*, and throughout the rest of the world she is, simply, the *Mona Lisa*.

The ambiguity of the sitter's expression, which is often described as 'enigmatic', is usually given as the reason for our enduring fascination with the painting. But the *Mona Lisa*'s smile once put a cheeky grin on other faces too – of the three conmen who, in 1911, not only sold forged copies of the masterpiece but stole the original, too. Those men were French art forger and former picture restorer Yves Chaudron, Argentinean trickster, self-styled marquis Eduardo de Valfierno and Italian burglar Vincenzo Perugia.

Chaudron and Valfierno had been partners in crime for many years. Their nefarious careers began at the turn of the century in South America where they would offer to steal a painting for a crooked dealer, who would sell it on to a client without too many questions being asked. This is how their amazing scam worked.

Chaudron and Valfierno would visit an art gallery in the guise of supposed art experts (which, in a way, they were). They would target a particular painting and chat with the gallery owner about its merits. On a second visit, they would return armed with a forgery of the 'target' painting, brilliantly executed by Chaudron. Again, he and Valfierno would engage the gallery owner in conversation and eventually ask the unsuspecting official if they could examine the work more closely. When it was taken down from the wall, the deceitful duo would cunningly line the back of the canvas with the forgery.

On their third visit to the gallery, they would have the crooked dealer in tow. He would be invited to make a surreptitious mark on the back of the painting that was to be stolen: he would, of course, be marking the back of the fake. On their fourth and final visit to the gallery, Chaudron and Valfierno would craftily remove the marked forgery. The gallery officials were never aware of their part in the confidence trick, since the genuine article remained in place. The crooked dealer, however, always greedily handed over the promised sum for the 'stolen' work of art.

If the dealer or the eventual purchaser of the forgery ever wondered why the original painting still hung on the gallery wall, Chaudron and Valfierno would let it be known that a copy of the original had taken its place while the theft was being investigated. In fact, as well as being great forgers, they were also great judges of human character. They knew that it was unlikely that the people tricked would ever realise that the copies they purchased were fakes. Even if they suspected it, their pride and vanity would generally persuade them that they were too smart to be duped. And, after all, if it ever dawned on the dealers or the clients that they had been conned, they could hardly go to the police to admit being part of the shady deal. Their reputations as art connoisseurs and honest traders was at stake!

Since Chaudron specialised in faking the work of Spanish artist Bartolemé Esteban Murillo, it did not take too many months before Argentina, where he and Valfierno were then operating, became flooded with phoney Murillos. They moved on to Mexico City, where they perfected their techniques, even providing specially printed 'newspaper cuttings' reporting on the supposed thefts of the works they had replicated and sold. When Mexico City became too hot for the crooks, they headed for Paris. There they naturally enough visited the world's most renowned art gallery, the Louvre Museum, and of course espied the world's most famous painting, the *Mona Lisa*.

The scam dreamed up by Yves Chaudron and Eduardo de Valfierno was of epic proportions. They realised they needed a third member for their gang, and recruited Vincenzo Perugia, an Italian burglar and small-time crook who had once worked in the Louvre as a handyman. He knew his way around the gallery and had even put the glass in the screen that protected Leonardo da Vinci's masterpiece from the public. Unbelievably, the gang of three then plotted to steal the *Mona Lisa*.

On Sunday, August 20, 1911, dressed as a workman, Perugia coolly wandered into the Louvre and secreted himself in the basement. After dark, he emerged from hiding and removed the *Mona Lisa* from the wall, discarded the frame and hid the painting (which measures just 77 cm by 53 cm (30 inch by 21 inch) under his smock. Within minutes he had vanished into the Parisian night. And by morning Chaudron and Valfierno had been handed the art world's ultimate prize.

The painting was discovered missing the following day, yet the police were not called because museum officials assumed that it had been taken to the Louvre's in-house studio for a scheduled photographic session for the creation of a new brochure. It wasn't until the Tuesday that the alarm was raised, police were called in and the embarrassing gap on the wall of the Louvre became a major news story worldwide.

One of the many theories surrounding its disappearance revolved around the renowned artist Pablo Picasso, who was said to have previously unknowingly purchased stolen artworks from a friend. It was believed that he might have also bought the stolen *Mona Lisa*. Detectives drew a blank but, refusing to abandon this strange line of inquiry, they arrested Picasso's friend, French poet Guillaume Apollinaire, and held him for a week on suspicion of selling the painting, before finally releasing him.

Meanwhile, the *Mona Lisa* was far away and, strangely, in perfectly safe hands. At the time they had stolen the painting, the gang already had several prospective clients lined up. For, although it would have been a simple task to sell the genuine *Mona Lisa*, the thieves had a more ambitious plan. They would sell the masterpiece not once but over and over again – and not one of the paintings they unloaded would be the original article. Before the year 1911 was out, no fewer than six American millionaires had each paid $300,000 for what each of them thought was da Vinci's masterpiece. It mattered little to them that the work had been stolen from the Louvre: greed overcame any feelings of guilt when seizing upon such a priceless work at such a knock-down price.

Chaudron and Valfierno made a little under $2 million selling their six expertly forged copies of the Louvre painting. But they never got the chance to dispose of the real thing. The newly hired member of the trio, Perugia, grew greedy and ran off to Italy with the real *Mona Lisa*. After two years in hiding, he finally tried to sell it.

On December 10, 1913, Perugia, using the alias Leonardo Vincenzo, entered the Florence offices of art dealer Alfredo Geri and told him he had the genuine *Mona Lisa* but that, as a self-proclaimed patriot, he believed the masterpiece belonged not in the Louvre but in an Italian museum. He wished to return it to Italy – but wanted 500,000 lire for his troubles. Initially highly sceptical, Geri agreed to view the painting the next day at Perugia's hotel room, where he arrived with his friend Giovanni Poggi, director of Florence's famous Uffizi Gallery. There, they watched in astonishment as Perugia removed the painting from the false bottom of an old trunk.

The two art experts told Perugia they must first check the authenticity of the painting before they could buy it. The dim thief gave Geri and Poggi permission to take the painting to a museum and, as he waited patiently in his hotel room, police pounced and arrested him. The trail then led to Yves Chaudron and Eduardo de Valfierno, and the three crooks found themselves in jail.

The *Mona Lisa* was returned to the Louvre where, behind thick glass panels, wired to several alarm systems, and under armed guard, the masterpiece remains to this day. However, one lingering doubt remains about the world's most famous painting. No fewer than 60 other alleged *Mona Lisas* have been catalogued in various corners of the world. And they are not all forgeries. Most are believed to be genuine and are attributed, if not to Leonardo da Vinci himself, then to his school of painting. So no one can be absolutely sure that the *Mona Lisa* hanging in the Louvre today is the one and only original. Can that be the reason for the lady's enigmatic smile?

CHAPTER 26

Prince of Parasites

Harry Benson was a fraudster whose fingers – and indeed, the rest of his body – were quite literally badly burned through his dodgy dealings. With his noble air and linguistic skills, Benson, the son of respectable Jewish parents but portraying himself as a member of European nobility, could easily be described as a prince among conmen. Benson always had an eye for the main chance. Born in England in 1848, he was fortunate enough to spend some of his educational years in Paris, giving him a cultural headstart and lots of confidence to mix with the rich, aristocratic and influential. It was this that provided a natural entrée to British society following the Franco-Prussian War of 1870.

His arrival on the London social scene coincided with the era of a sudden and inexplicable upsurge in fraud cases. In the 1870s, Scotland Yard found itself under intense pressure to catch these scoundrels, not least because their gullible victims tended to be the rich and influential. Fleecing the wealthy was easy money for a skilled operator, and they didn't come any more skilful than Harry Benson.

Benson called himself the Count de Montagu when he returned to England and met with the Lord Mayor of London. He introduced himself as the mayor of the small French town of Chateaudun, which had been nearly demolished in the recent war and explained that he was collecting funds for the poor and needy of his town. The Lord Mayor gave him £1,000 but hardly had Benson pocketed the cash than his forged receipt was spotted and he was arrested and convicted of fraud. He was sentenced to a year in London's notorious Newgate Prison. It was an experience so loathsome to him, and so far removed from the somewhat privileged existence he had always enjoyed, that Benson did not have the backbone to accept his incarceration. He tried to commit suicide in the most horrific manner, attempting to incinerate himself on his prison mattress. The flames left him half-crippled and, after spending some time in a wheelchair, he found himself restricted to walking only with the aid of crutches.

Released in July 1873, Benson immediately changed his name to J.H. Yonge and advertised his services as a multilingual secretary. He was later to use many other aliases while conducting new swindles, including Count Yonge, G.H. Yonge, Hugh Montgomery and George Washington Morton. His newly-found accomplice was 23-year-old William Kurr, a clever, young conman who was in the business of setting up dummy companies that dealt in turf betting and whose living was made through his gambling swindles. Kurr's usual method was to place bets for clients at a race meeting and then vanish with the proceeds of any big win. It was a primitive technique but effective enough.

The two men quickly got the measure of each other and soon Benson was persuading Kurr to try more sophisticated scams. Benson enacted the role of a celebrated horse race gambler who claimed he was so successful that, whenever he bet on a race, the odds dropped on his favourite. In this way, Kurr claimed, they could manipulate odds and produce enormous profits for investors. Thousands of gullible racegoers poured money into the fake firms, enriching Benson and Kurr but producing little profit. The swindlers would fold one firm after having sold off its paper assets to another and continue this process, so that their gambling company schemes presented an incredible labyrinth of legal documents.

The two tricksters began publishing a newspaper, *Le Sport*, which comprised mainly British racing articles translated into French. It was delivered free to selected French aristocrats with a keen interest in the turf. Those who scanned its pages read how a professional British punter called Mr G.H. Yonge had such an incredibly successful track record that many bookies cut the odds whenever they did business with him. Strangely enough, some of the aristocrats soon began receiving letters from Mr Yonge in which they were asked to act as his agent in laying bets. He could not, he explained, use his real name because bookmakers wouldn't give him decent odds. All his agents had to do was receive a cheque, forward it to a certain bookmaker in their own name and return the winnings to Mr Yonge. In return the agent would receive a five per cent commission.

One trusting, aristocratic Frenchwoman, the Comtesse de Goncourt, found this an acceptable arrangement. Benson, who had recovered from his crippling wounds and was now walking about with the aid of a cane, invited the wealthy Parisienne into the betting scheme by which she expected to make amazing profits. The comtesse would mail Mr Yonge's cheque for several hundred pounds, receive back thousands in winnings and pocket £50 or so commission for herself. After a few trial runs, she became so convinced that Yonge was a gambling genius that she asked him if he would mind very much investing £10,000 of her own money as he saw fit. Unfortunately the comtesse did not cotton on to the simple truth that Yonge's 'bookmaker' was, like Yonge himself, just another of Benson's aliases. In addition, she gave Benson and Kurr £1,000 and then another £10,000, believing she would soon be realising ten times that amount through the bets placed by them on her behalf. She never saw her £10,000 again – though, naively, she continued to entrust Benson with her money while she waited for the 'big win'.

A new cast of shady characters now entered this bubbling cauldron of deceit. They were senior police officers with Scotland Yard – but far from upholding the law they were intent on bending it.

Nathaniel Druscovich and Chief Inspector John Meiklejohn were specifically assigned to the task of stamping out betting frauds. Their stock in trade was to hobnob with 'narks', usually petty criminals who kept themselves out of jail by passing on useful criminal intelligence. The use of informers was, and remains, a vital part of police work but there is often a fine line between professional agreements and corruption. The taking of bribes was a great temptation to an officer of Victorian England, who earned a meagre £5 6s.2d. a year. So when Chief Inspector John Meiklejohn was offered cash by William Kurr in return for dropping investigations into Kurr's criminal dealings, he readily accepted.

Meiklejohn's friend, Chief Inspector Druscovich, admitted to him that he had money problems, so he also became a recipient of Harry Benson's largesse. All the conman wanted in return, he said, was a little advance warning of any plan Scotland Yard might have to arrest him. The deal was struck and soon a third detective, Chief Inspector William Palmer, was brought onto Benson's payroll.

All of these Scotland Yard detectives were in charge of the Continental Branch of Investigation, which dealt with violations of the Betting Act. When warrants for either Kurr or Benson were issued by their irate victims, the officers warned their criminal associates or 'lost' the warrants, receiving considerable pay-offs for these services.

Not long after the corrupt circle was in place, Meiklejohn delivered a warning to Benson that detectives were snapping at his heels. A Chief Inspector Clarke had been assigned to close down bogus bookmakers and he was very interested in the firm of Gardner & Co, a front company used by Kurr, Benson and their cohorts. One of those associates was a swindler called Walters, whom Clarke had encountered while he was in the process of smashing another gang.

With impressive nerve, Benson, using his 'Yonge' alias, wrote to the officer inviting him to visit his palatial country home at Shanklin, on the Isle of Wight. He explained that he had some useful criminal intelligence but that he couldn't get up to London because he was crippled. Intrigued, Clarke agreed and at the meeting was informed by 'Mr Yonge' that Walters had been boasting of success in bribing Clarke; worse, that he still had a letter penned by the chief inspector which proved the allegation. Clarke had indeed once written to Walters and he now acknowledged that his words were open to misinterpretation.

This entire episode, daringly risky as it seemed, was cooked up by Benson to try to warn Clarke off. So accustomed was he to dealing with bent cops that Benson no doubt believed Clarke too would fall into line. But his ruse failed. The officer reported to his superiors that Yonge was probably a crook – and, with uncorrupted Scotland Yard officers watching his every move, Benson's next blatant scam signalled the beginning of the end of his swindling career.

Instead of being content with the money he and Kurr had so far wrung out of the Comtesse de Goncourt, they again contacted her with the offer of a unique investment opportunity if she could raise £30,000. She swallowed their line but told them that she would have to consult her lawyer in order to convert a number of assets into ready cash. The lawyer, hearing what his gullible client had been up to, contacted the authorities in England.

Scotland Yard assigned one of their top detectives to run down the conmen. But it was the dodgy Druscovich, who was able to tip them off that the game was up. Benson, Kurr and the rest of the gang pulled £16,000 in cash out of a Bank of England account and headed for Scotland in the hope their trail would go cold. It didn't. Druscovich was dispatched to arrest them but, before he did, he sent a telegram warning Benson that he was on his way. For this service, he and the other two 'bent' officers received £500 apiece for their trouble.

Senior detectives at Scotland Yard were by now growing frustrated and puzzled at their inability to nail the Benson gang. At first, it did not occur to them that men within their own ranks had been 'nobbled', even when Meiklejohn was spotted hobnobbing with the crooks at their Scottish hideaway in Bridge of Allan, near Stirling, he talked himself out of trouble by claiming he didn't realise they were the wanted scoundrels.

Eventually, Benson fled to Holland and Kurr returned to London, where Druscovich was again asked to track him down. Knowing perfectly well where to find him, the policeman went first to Kurr. 'I have to arrest someone,' he explained, 'but preferably not you.' Arrogant Kurr simply shrugged and told him to go ahead and arrest him, believing he could bluff his way out of any charge. Druscovich refused, however, being justifiably nervous that, if Kurr or Benson were questioned, the entire web of police corruption would be exposed. The policeman returned to Scotland Yard empty-handed. Other officers were not so lax. They followed up the manhunt and arrested Kurr in his pub in London's Islington.

By now, Benson had also been traced, to Rotterdam where Scotland Yard had already alerted Dutch police to the possibility that the conman, perhaps travelling under one of his many aliases, would turn up on their doorstep. As the heat increased, Benson tried to use a £100 banknote which police knew was one of a batch he had withdrawn some weeks earlier. The Dutch arrested him and, in yet another act of irony, Druscovich, the detective most involved in Benson's fraudulent empire, found himself being sent to Rotterdam to arrest his criminal paymaster. He did so, at last realising he could do his crooked benefactor no more favours.

The rest of the gang was duly rounded up. Benson and Kurr were put on trial at the Old Bailey in April 1877 charged with fraud and forgery. Benson was given a fifteen-year prison term, and Kurr, his brother Frederick Kurr, and a man named Bale were given ten-year terms. Others in their gang of fraudsters also received long sentences.

Within hours of their reception at London's Millbank prison, both Benson and Kurr asked to see the governor and spilled the beans on the network of corruption they had established within the very heart of Scotland Yard. Just as the corrupt detectives had feared, they tried to bargain for lesser sentences by exposing the police officers who had been on their payroll. Meiklejohn, Druscovich and Palmer were tried and convicted of conspiring to pervert the course of justice, and all were sentenced to the maximum two years hard labour – mild terms compared to that meted out to Benson and Kurr. Clarke was acquitted and, although forcibly retired, was permitted to keep his police pension. When the jailed officers were released at the end of their sentences, Meiklejohn set himself up in business as a private eye, while Palmer used his life savings to open a pub. Of Druscovich's fate, nothing is known.

Benson and Kerr both got time off their sentences for good behaviour. They teamed up again, this time as mining company consultants in America, and soon the hapless European public were being offered shares in mines that didn't exist. Benson was again arrested and served two years in a Swiss prison. His last great con was in Mexico, selling bogus tickets for concerts by the celebrated Italian-American opera singer Adelina Patti.

Benson had met the famous soprano on board a ship taking her to New York, bowing to her as she was about to disembark. She thought him to be one of the delegation meeting her at the Manhattan dock and allowed him to take her arm, escorting her down the gangplank. To the New York officials greeting her, Benson appeared to be one of the prima donna's entourage. This, of course, was Benson's intent. He quickly set himself up as Patti's New York agent and he collected a $20,000 advance from Mexican officials who thought they were booking Patti for a concert in Mexico City. Benson managed to flee the ensuing police hunt and again arrived in America, where he spent several more years pursuing his criminal activities. He was eventually arrested and ended up in the Tombs prison in New York City.

But just like that very first jail sentence, Benson could not bear the thought of living a life behind bars. He finally achieved what he had attempted almost two decades before in Newgate Prison – committing suicide by breaking his back in a leap off a 40ft prison balcony.

CHAPTER 27

'A Likeable Bastard'

Peter Clarence Foster is, in the words of an old school friend, 'a likeable bastard'. An affable but, at first sight, unimpressive Australian, Foster is nevertheless one of the greatest confidence tricksters of all time. Whether chizzling small traders or duping governments, he is a master at his craft.

Foster, it has to be conceded, is an engaging rogue. He somehow has the gift of being able to persuade even the most sceptical and cynical individuals to part with their natural caution – and ultimately their money. And it is all done so seemingly effortlessly, which, of course, is the mark of a great confidence trickster.

Foster's home territory is Australia's Gold Coast, that strip of high-rise beachside high-life that glitters on the Pacific shores of Queensland and is the holiday haunt of bikini-clad beauties and bleached-haired surfers. Foster could have been one of the latter but his ambition drove him, at an early age, away from the golden beaches and into the hotel bars of the town of Surfers Paradise. He could have become a respectable businessman, rich through honest dealings, but that was not his way. 'It's not that he couldn't make a living out of running a legitimate business; it was just more fun for him to try to beat the system,' according to his former classmate at Aquinas Catholic College. He recalled young Foster being 'heavily into horse racing' and said the family once returned from a holiday in the Philippines with 15-year-old Peter laden down with fake designer watches to sell at school.

That was the start of his life as a conman. In that nefarious career, he has hoodwinked get-rich-quick merchants, charity workers, prisoners in jail, and warders in charge of them, shopkeepers, hotels, credit card companies, beautiful models, hard-headed businessmen, lawyers and politicians. As the pinnacle of his career, he even sucked the British Prime Minister and his family into his web of deceit. And all done so effortlessly, with a cheeky smile, a merry quip, a glass of champagne in hand.

But that was all ahead of him when the fresh-faced Foster left his Queensland school and launched himself as an entrepreneur. The start of this career was not auspicious, however. His first venture was promoting pop concerts and boxing bouts but he fell foul of the law in 1983 when he was fined £75,000 for trying to defraud an insurance company out of £40,000. The following year he was declared bankrupt after trying to market a 'magic' method of quitting smoking.

With his reputation sullied in Australia, he sought a broader stage for his grand game and in January 1986 and, at the age of 24, he flew to Britain seeking to ride to riches on someone else's coat-tails. His unwitting target was the country's most desired pin-up, Samantha Fox, famous at the time for her nubile body which graced the pages of calendars, posters and tabloid newspapers. He wooed and won her, not just to make himself the most envied man in Britain but also because he needed a celebrity sponsor to launch his latest 'miracle' slimming potion, Bai Lin Tea. He persuaded Sam to promote the dodgy brew, and over the next ten years the lovebirds travelled the world in style, from Australia to Tokyo to Africa's Safari country. He bought her jewellery, a sports car, a magnificent home and claimed to be deeply in love with her. The cheat was seeing other women on the side, however, and when Sam found out, she dumped him, later referring to him only as 'the Rat'.

Meanwhile, Foster had made untold millions out of selling Bai Lin Tea franchises in Britain, taking £5,000 from each of about 100 would-be distributors. However, when the product was labelled a sham by TV hostess Esther Rantzen on her top-rated show *That's Life*, the pyramid selling scam collapsed with debts of £700,000 and Foster's company, Slimweight, ended up in voluntary liquidation.

Foster soon bounced back with a new diet scam, hiring Britain's 1998 Young Slimmer of the Year, Michelle Deakin, to back his next product. Nineteen-year-old Michelle was persuaded to launch the 'Deakin Diet', claiming that she had won her title by taking Foster's cheap pills filled with guar gum. The naive Liverpool girl fell for his soft sell after he wooed her with champagne parties, rides in his Rolls Royce and flights in a private jet. But her claim to have lost weight through the conman's pills was shown to be a transparent lie. As Foster faced trial on trades description charges and the Bai Lin venture collapsed, he fled to Australia in 1987.

Back home in Surfers Paradise he was reunited with his mother Louise Polleti, long divorced from the conman's father, hotel owner Clarence 'Clarrie' Foster, who died in 1998. Many of those who know Peter Foster believe his mother is the only woman he is really close to. 'She is a fearsomely strong character and has total influence over him,' says an Australian journalist who knows them. 'She treats him as her little boy and, to her, he can do no wrong.' An ex-friend of the family adds: 'Louise runs Peter's life for him and he hardly makes a move without his mother's say-so. When they are together they bicker all the time but when apart they are on the phone constantly.'

In 1989 Foster turned up in California, establishing a base in Beverly Hills to peddle another useless slimming product, Chow Lo Tea. Having run up huge advertising debts and serving four months in jail for false claims, he again went on the run. After persuading the Australian consulate in Los Angeles to issue him with a passport, he flew to the Caribbean, then to Australia – much to the annoyance of Los Angeles city attorney Jim Hahn who described him as 'a con artist peddling snake oil'.

Back again in Queensland, Foster devised Biometrics Contour Treatment which he claimed shrank girls' thighs. He sold a string of franchises before (and after) the Trade Practices Commission banned his business, accusing him of misleading and deceptive conduct.

Foster was now literally running out of places to which to run. In 1994 he returned to Britain, supposedly 'to wipe the slate clean' over his previous UK diet scams, including Bai Lin Tea, and pay two outstanding penalties of about £25,000 each, one against himself and one against his mother as chairman of one his companies. He paid only his own – which, as we shall see, was to cause his mother some problems.

On this return visit to Britain, he very publicly kissed and made up with Sam Fox, saying that 'letting her go was the biggest mistake I ever made'. According to Foster, he resumed his affair with her and even planned marriage – claims which shocked Fox fans because since their last romance she had given up nude modelling, started a singing career and a lesbian relationship and had become a born-again Christian. Whether or not his nuptial plans for Ms Fox were genuine, the playboy's hidden agenda was to involve her in his next diet scam. Sam was having none of it and the rekindled romance quickly fizzled out.

Other products were dreamed up. There was Thigh Tone 1, then Body Right Pro which Pamela Anderson, star of American TV series *Baywatch*, was conned into backing. A video was made with a shaky hand-held camera in which Pamela appeared to support the product, and this was about to be used to persuade British punters to buy distributorships when police again pounced. Foster was remanded in custody on the earlier Deakin Diet offences under the Trades Description Act.

At Liverpool Crown Court in January 1996 he was told by the judge: 'I have formed a very unfavourable view of you as someone whose champagne lifestyle meant that as long as you cut a dash or make a splash, you were happy to do so. It may fairly be said that the party is now over.' In fact, the party was only just beginning, although it did not look like it at the time to Peter Foster. Sentenced to two years' jail, after which he was to be deported, he was incarcerated in ultra-tough Walton Prison, Liverpool, and later the fortress-like Winson Green, Birmingham. His mother, Louise, immediately flew from Australia to comfort her son in jail but never got past Heathrow Airport. When her plane touched down, she was arrested for non-payment of her £25,000 fine. Because her son had gambled away the money set aside to clear her debt, she spent four weeks, including

Christmas, in London's Holloway women's prison. She was eventually freed when her other child, Jill, organised a whip-round back in Queensland.

Forgiven by his doting mother, Peter launched an appeal which reduced his two-year sentence to eighteen months so that, with remission, he needed to serve only nine months. Happily for him, he was moved to Sudbury open prison, Derbyshire, where his tales of sun, fun and sex in the fast lane made his fellow inmates green with envy – then red with rage when he took some of them for a ride with his phoney promises.

Foster was regularly allowed out with a prison officer to raise funds for the jail's own anti-drugs charity, Outreach, but in August 1996 he walked through the gates and never returned. Why he should go on the run only ten days before he was due to be freed was, at first, a mystery. The answer, it was later revealed, was that Foster feared fresh fraud charges were being prepared against him over his Thigh Tone activities.

His disappearance from Sudbury was a severe embarrassment for prison officers who had trusted him to work outside the jail on their Outreach charity venture. It was also damaging to former inmates whom he had persuaded to work for him on his next planned diet scam and who now feared their parole would be cancelled. And it was financially disastrous to businessmen, whom he had already persuaded to hand over money for the project, including, astonishingly, a fellow prisoner at Sudbury who had given him £13,000.

Finally, it could have been highly embarrassing for Samantha Fox, because Foster had spent his time in jail penning his 'prison diaries'. In this racy version of his life story, he claimed that he had reformed and was now a man of honour. But the diaries went on to describe in intimate detail many of the sexual delights in which he and Fox had indulged. The diaries had to be salacious because he planned to sell them to a newspaper and then a book publisher. Happily for Sam Fox, he failed to complete them before going on the run.

Fugitive Foster first fled to Ireland and then to Australia, where he was again jailed for five months for entering the country on a false passport and inducing witnesses to give false evidence. The judge in the case at Southport District Court, on the Gold Coast, appeared to sympathise with the conman, as ever in contrite and charming mood. Judge John Newton praised his initiative and said: 'As an entrepreneur you have attempted to develop a number of business projects which seem to offer a great deal of scope for success.' The judge even offered his 'best wishes' for the jailbird's next supposed endeavour, Outreach Australia, a project to teach children the dangers of drugs and keep them from a life of crime – an idea he had conveniently borrowed from the warders he had conned at Sudbury prison. For his part, Foster promised, tongue presumably firmly in cheek, that he would 'endeavour to use my period of incarceration constructively and for the benefit of the community as a whole'. Predictably, as soon as he was released he went back to his old tricks.

So why does Peter Foster bother to take the harsh and rocky route to riches? Why not settle for an honest life as a legitimate businessman, as the Australian judge had suggested when he described the fraudster as an 'entrepreneur'? The answer is supplied by Foster himself, who once told a buddy: 'The money's great but the buzz comes from knowing you've pulled off the sting. It's better than sex.'

That motivation is in the character of many of the great confidence tricksters of history. For it is the thrill of the sting that drives them, even more than the ill-gotten rewards. It is the mastery of mind games that makes a conman tick. And on the evidence of former friends, acquaintances, business partners and lovers, Foster is the most persuasive conman they have ever met. As many of them admit, he's a 'likeable guy'.

A lawyer who once had dealings with him revealed that, before a visit by Foster, he would arrange for a secretary to call him out of his office on a pretext. 'I had to leave the room and shake my head,' he said. 'I reckon I'm a fairly cynical man and experience has made me a good judge of character but if I listened to Foster for too long, even I started to believe him.'

A former business partner said: 'He has a hypnotic effect on people he's trying to sell himself to. He never has any trouble getting the promise of backing from normally hard-headed businessmen. His effect on more trusting people can be devastating. He'll take their money, cheat them and ruin their lives without a qualm. He doesn't stab them in the back; he smiles them in the back.'

Another ex-partner who got to know how the conman worked says that he will always bounce back. 'Peter is a great collector of information and always plans for the future. His schemes have turned to dust so often in the past that he has learned always to have a contingency plan. He's a hoarder of damaging information that might one day be useful to him.'

So, while appearing not to have a care in the world, Foster will be coolly, cunningly, perfectly planning a plot to ensnare his victim – and the next one, and the next one. No detail is too small and no target too big for him.

So it beggared belief that when Peter Foster next arrived in Britain, he was allowed to get close to the highest seat of power in the land: to trick his way into the confidence of Number 10 Downing Street and to be on first-name terms with the Prime Minister's family. It was the pinnacle of his career as a conman.

Foster made front-page news day after day in late 2002 after the fraudster embroiled Premier Tony Blair and his wife Cherie, a leading barrister, in serious allegations of political sleaze. It emerged that Foster had become the lover of Cherie's closest confidante, her indispensable fashion and lifestyle guru Carole Caplin, and had taken on the role of Mrs Blair's part-time financial adviser. He had used his negotiating skills to purchase two apartments for the Blairs at a bargain price in an upmarket development in Bristol.

It seemed an unbelievable lapse of common sense for Tony Blair to have allowed a conman such control over his family's private affairs. But strenuous denials from Downing Street were soon seen to be a smokescreen as documents proved the closeness of Foster's relationship with the Blairs: at the same time he was using it to entice investors to sink money into his latest dubious slimming venture.

The scam was devilishly clever. Foster had known of Caplin's connection to the Prime Minister before even meeting her. She was a regular visitor to Downing Street and had even holidayed with the Blairs abroad. She conducted Cherie in fitness workouts, alternative therapy sessions and even chose her clothes. Within three days of Foster engineering an introduction to Caplin at a trendy Chelsea coffee bar in July 2002, the 39-year-old conman and the 42-year-old former topless model were lovers. 'She's quite a babe,' Foster told a pal, 'but more importantly, she knows the Blairs.'

Soon he was boasting to investors in his new company Renuelle that he was on target to secure the PM's support for a healthy lifestyle programme aimed at schools. The Children's Education Programme would be a national tour organised by Renuelle to warn youngsters about the dangers of obesity. With government backing, Foster knew it would win Renuelle instant credibility, enabling him to market his latest quack diet pills, Trimit, through a network of franchisees, some of whom had already paid his company between £25,000 and £75,000.

Meanwhile, Foster had so ingratiated himself with Cherie Blair that she had allowed him to handle the purchase of two £297,000 apartments for her one for the use of her eighteen-year-old student son Euan and the other as an investment. The wheeler-dealer invoked the Blairs' name to haggle down the price of the properties by £69,000 and arranged to pick up the legal bill for the purchases. The fact that these negotiations on behalf of the Blairs were being enacted only three months after Foster first met Carole Caplin is an indication of just how swiftly the conman is able to insinuate himself into the lives of his victims.

When news of the property deal leaked out, Downing Street spin doctors went into overdrive, playing down the connection between the convicted conman and the Prime Minister's wife. But protestations from Number 10 were silenced by the record of a string of emails that had already passed between Foster and Mrs Blair at the time of the negotiations in October.

Conveniently released to a newspaper 'from a source in Australia', they made dynamite reading. 'We weren't looking to buy the property but steal it,' Foster told Cherie. Another email read: 'I have spoken to (a property manager) and he will jump through hoops for you. I have reduced his fee. I will keep the pressure on him to perform in double-quick time.' And cosily: 'Let me know if I can be of service. Your pleasure is my purpose – Peter'. Signing herself Cherie, she replied: 'I cannot thank you enough, Peter, for taking over these negotiations for me. I really appreciate it.' Other emails assured him that 'we certainly are on the same wavelength' and 'you're a star'.

The scandal was seen as so dangerous by the British government that, in an unprecedented move, Cherie Blair was forced to take the stage for a televised address to the nation in which, her voice breaking with emotion, she attempted to win the country's sympathy by portraying herself as a normal working mother trying to cope with a busy life. 'I'm not superwoman,' she declared. 'The reality of my daily life is that I'm juggling a lot of balls in the air: trying to be a good wife and mother, trying to be the Prime Minister's consort at home and abroad, a barrister and a charity worker — and sometimes some of the balls get dropped.' At one point she wept as she explained that she was (somehow) trying to protect her son by negotiating for the apartments but the verdict of most newspapers the following day was that hers was a sob story rather than the proper explanation expected of a tough £300,000-a-year leading barrister.

In the midst of this furore, Carole Caplin, revealed that she had been pregnant by Foster but had lost the baby. Much later, Foster was outrageously to claim that, having checked his diary, he rather felt that it may not have been he who had made Carole pregnant but Tony Blair. At the time, however, the conman had appeared genuinely supportive and had declared himself proud at the prospect of being a dad.

That was certainly the stance he took when Carole bravely (or foolishly) invited TV cameras into her home to film what turned out to be her boyfriend's last days in Britain. In the documentary, *The Conman, His Lover and the Prime Minister's*

Wife, Foster spoke about the storm over the Blairs' apartments, saying: 'I think Cherie has handled a bad situation atrociously and she let it get out of hand.' Asked if she had lied, he added: 'Yeah, yeah, she has.' An even more uncomfortable piece of viewing for Downing Street was when Tony Blair left a midnight message on Miss Caplin's answer machine, beginning: 'Hi, it's Tony calling.'

Throughout this period, Foster was fighting a legal battle against deportation back to Australia, which he claimed Cherie Blair was helping him overturn. Indeed, his case papers were faxed to Downing Street for Cherie's perusal. With time running out, and with impatient Trimit pill investors snapping at his heels for repayment of their stake money, Foster left Britain for Dublin to join his mother briefly before being finally deported from there to Australia. His parting shot to the Blairs was: 'Some say power corrupts and maybe power changes people.'

The person who changed most, however, was Peter Foster. Having quit Britain in a fit of self-pity, he brightened up when he hit the Gold Coast and threw himself into a round of carousing with his old mates. His vows of undying love for Carole Caplin were soon forgotten as he romped with two shapely new girlfriends. In a Surfers Paradise bar in March 2003, he was seen to take a call from Carole on his mobile phone, speaking earnestly to her for a few minutes before ending the conversation with the words: 'Trust me, Carole' – then turning back to the semi-clad blonde on his lap!

Apart from the announcement in 2004 of a 'tell all' autobiography (that predictably never materialised), nothing much was heard of Peter Clarence Foster for a few years. But he was quietly hatching fresh plans to separate the gullible from their hard-earned money. Says his ex-associate: 'He will do anything to advance himself and will sacrifice anyone else along the way. He is convinced that eventually his destiny is to be a leader on the world stage. He told me his long-term aim was to find a small country, probably among the Pacific islands, and offer his expertise to its leader to boost that nation's economy. He would do this for nothing in return for being granted ambassadorial status, so that he could hobnob with world politicians and travel the globe with diplomatic immunity.'

The boastful conversation was prophetic, as was proved when Foster was next in the news in October 2006 when he was arrested in Fiji, where he had been living and working as a property developer. He had also been acting as a consultant to one of the Pacific nation's political parties. On the run over fraud-related charges, Foster, clad only in his underpants, jumped off a bridge on the outskirts of the capital, Suva, but was picked up by a police launch.

A month later, a trusting judge freed him on bail, despite warnings that he was a 'huge flight risk' – which soon proved to be the case. In January 2007 Foster persuaded an Australian yacht crew to ferry him out of Suva, and he was next seen wading ashore on an isolated beach on the neighbouring island nation of Vanatu: he was stripped to the waist, carrying only a pair of sandals and a plastic bag with his possessions.

Jailed for entering the country illegally, he was deported three weeks later and flown to Queensland. There, he faced charges of money-laundering, and in December 2007 he was again imprisoned for forging documents relating to a $Aust 300,000 loan from the Bank of the Federated States of Micronesia, which he had transferred to Australia to repay credit card debts and to pay his girlfriend's rent. In February 2008, the Court of Appeal in Brisbane dismissed his plea for a reduction in the sentence, his lawyers unsuccessfully arguing that his four-and-a-half-year jail term had been excessive and that the original judge had placed too much emphasis on his criminal history.

That final, failed plea typified Foster because, as a former friend said: 'Every time something goes wrong, Peter believes he is the victim.' In any case, it would be difficult to over-emphasise the conman's criminal history, since it covers crimes and terms of imprisonment in Europe, North America, Australasia and Micronesia.

Early in his disreputable career, Foster boasted: 'Being a conman is one of the most prestigious professions you can pursue. Every day crackled with excitement as I made millions, models and mayhem.' More recently, he seemed to have changed his mind. When asked by Melbourne's *Age* newspaper whether he still called himself a conman, he replied: 'International man of mischief is clever and perhaps more accurate.' But someone has to be holder of the inglorious title 'The World's Greatest Living Conman' and that dishonour deservedly belongs to Peter Clarence Foster.

CHAPTER 28

The Big Fat Liar

If Peter Foster *(see previous chapter)* can lay claim to the dishonourable title 'The World's Greatest Living Conman', then Arthur Orton can be discredited with the title of 'The World's Worst Conman Ever'. Yet, by bravado and determination, the two sharpest tools of a confidence trickster's trade, Orton came within a hair's breadth of succeeding in one of the most far-fetched frauds of all time. Such is the gullibility of those who are ever-willing to be convinced by the implausible, the incredible or the outright absurd.

Orton was a fat, obnoxious butcher who succeeded in conning one of Britain's premier families into believing that he was their long-lost heir. At the time, it was the greatest fraud case ever heard, and also the longest-running legal action in history. During its course, the fraudster had to prove that his real identity was not Arthur Orton but Sir Roger Tichborne – whereas his real name wasn't even Arthur Orton!

To explain this most complicated of plots, one needs to start the story with the genuine Sir Roger Tichborne. Born in 1830, he was the elder son of Englishman James Tichborne and his French wife Henriette, a wealthy Roman Catholic couple who lived in Paris and had four children, only two of whom, both boys, survived. When James Tichborne's brother, the tenth baronet, died without leaving a son and heir, Roger suddenly leaped to next in line to take the title.

Roger, a feeble lad prone to asthma attacks, was idolized by his mother who spoiled him and gave in to his every whim. His father, irritated by Henriette's obsessive love for her son, was anxious the boy should be whipped into shape, so sent him to a strict English boarding school, the Jesuit college Stonyhurst, in Lancashire. Four years later his father secured a commission for Roger in the Sixth Dragoon Guards, where he was nicknamed 'Small Cock' – for reasons that will become clear.

Roger was now in his early twenties and he turned to more romantic interests. He fell in love with his cousin, Katherine Doughty, but their romance was doomed. The Roman Catholic Church did not allow first cousins to marry and Katherine's family did not consider Roger a suitable match. Her father, Sir Edward Doughty, forbade the two to meet for three years. Sir Edward told them that if they obeyed his instructions and their feelings were still strong for each other when the three years had passed, he would reconsider. He would even try to obtain dispensation from the Catholic Church to allow them to marry.

Roger and Katherine reluctantly agreed to comply with her father's wishes. They bade a tearful farewell, never realising it was the last time they would ever see each other. When Katherine had gone, Roger sat down and wrote a moving letter to her. It read: 'I make on this day a promise, if I marry my cousin Katherine Doughty this year, or before three years are over at the latest, to build a church or chapel at Tichborne to the Holy Virgin in thanksgiving for the protection which she has thrown over us, and praying God that our wishes may be fulfilled.' To prove his intent, Roger made a copy of the letter and gave it for safe-keeping to a trusted friend, Vincent Gosport. He then resigned his commission and boarded a boat bound for South America.

Roger spent ten months trying to forget Katherine, scraping a living in Chile and Argentina. He then decided to head for the United States, and in 1854 the 24-year-old joined a small British trader, the *Bella*, leaving Rio de Janeiro for New York. He was never to complete the journey. The *Bella* went down in fierce Atlantic storms. The only trace left of her was the logbook. There were no listed survivors. Roger's mother was overcome with grief at hearing the news. She blamed her husband for sending their beloved son away. Never recovering from the loss, James Tichborne died soon afterwards. Three years later, Roger Tichborne was officially declared dead, and the family estate and title was passed to Roger's young brother, Alfred.

Henriette felt the whole family was cursed. She had lost three of her children and her husband. But in her tortured mind, she believed that somehow her darling boy Roger would one day return to her, and she began an international search for him. She placed advertisements in newspapers everywhere, from South America to Australia, asking for information about her son. On August 5, 1865, a front-page advert appeared in the Sydney newspaper *The Australasian*: 'A handsome reward will be given to any person who can furnish such information as will discover the fate of Roger Charles Tichborne...the son of Sir James Tichborne (now deceased) and heir to all his estates.'

A copy of the newspaper fell into the hands of Arthur Orton, a semi-literate butcher from Wagga Wagga, in the Australian Outback. Under the assumed name of Thomas Castro, this ne'er-do-well had emigrated from the East End of London to escape his creditors and had settled in Australia with a wife and two young children.

Orton's poor literacy prevented him fully understanding the meaning of the advert, but when it was explained to him, he decided to target the Tichborne family with a dastardly deception – seeking not only someone else's fortune but a baronetcy too. Clutching the advertisement, Orton made his way to the office of a local lawyer, William Gibbes, and told him the incredible story that, although he was living under the name of Thomas Castro, he was in fact, the missing Roger Charles Tichborne. As proof, he showed the lawyer a pipe carved with the initials R.C.T. Gibbes was taken in by his story, and wrote to Henriette in Paris, telling her that her son might indeed still be alive.

Henriette was overjoyed, replying immediately. She begged to learn more, asking that 'Roger' write to her himself. With some difficulty, Orton, in January 1866, penned a letter addressed to 'My dear Mother' which went on: 'The delay which has taken place since my last Letter, Dated 22nd April, 1854, Makes it very difficult to commence this letter. I deeply regret the truble and anxiety I must have cause you by not writing before. Of one thing rest Assured that although I have been in A humble condition of Life I have never let any act disgrace you or my Family. I have been poor man and nothing worse.'

The reply from the Dowager Lady Tichborne arrived in April. Her state of mind while writing it may well have been influenced by the fact that, only three days earlier, her youngest son Alfred had died of drink, leaving his baby son Henry as the twelfth baronet. She wrote: 'My dear and beloved Roger, I hope you will not refuse to come back to your poor afflicted mother. I have had the great misfortune to lose your poor dear father and lately I have lost my beloved son Alfred. I am now alone in this world of sorrow.'

A regular correspondence began between mother and 'son'. Henriette, in her desperation to believe her son was still alive, apparently did not question the nature of Orton's letters, ignoring friends when they pointed out that the degree of literacy in them conflicted with the expensive education Roger had received at Stonyhurst. Henriette wrote to Orton to tell him to hasten to Sydney, where he would receive instructions for his passage to Europe.

Thus, with £20,000 borrowed on the strength of his new-found fortune, Orton arrived in Sydney and encountered the first hurdles between his outrageous claims and the Tichborne inheritance. In the city, he was interviewed by Francis Turville, private secretary to the Governor of New South Wales, and an old friend of the Tichborne family. Turville reported back that Orton was a strange character, 'dirty enough', with 'his English too a little butchery at times'. Yet his manner displayed so little effort towards convincing anyone he was an English aristocrat that Turville described him as 'the reverse of an imposter'.

Orton's next barrier was in convincing an old family servant of the Tichborne family by the name of Bogle. The black retainer was either so excited at being reunited with young Roger, or had been promised some reward in maintaining the pretence, that he confirmed to Henriette that her son was indeed alive and well. Thus Orton, accompanied by his family and the faithful Bogle, set sail for England.

Seeking to avoid an early meeting with Henriette, Orton first headed for the Tichborne family seat in Hampshire, where he failed dismally to convince the locals that he was the long-lost Roger Tichborne. Even the village blacksmith saw through him, saying; 'If you are Sir Roger, you've changed from a racehorse to a carthorse!' The blacksmith last remembered Roger Tichborne as a slim man with a long pointed face, sallow complexion and straight, black hair. Yet here before him was a man with a florid face, greasy waved hair and weighing over 20 stone.

Roger's old tutor, Henri Chatillon, also saw through Orton straight away. He could not accept that the skinny little runt he had once taught could ever have become such an obese, uncouth person. Not only that, this man was much older than Roger would have been. He bore no tattoo on his arm as Roger had. And he did not understand French, the language Roger had been so expertly tutored in.

Orton was not to be put off. He travelled to Paris determined to convince the one person who really mattered, Henriette Tichborne herself. The reunion between mother and 'son' took place in the hotel where Orton was ensconced – with the excuse that he was too ill to travel further. The lonely Henriette, now aged, frail and confused, did not question Orton's plea that the room be darkened because of his ailments, nor that he covered his tearful face with a handkerchief. 'Oh my dear Roger, is it you?' she asked. 'Oh Mama', cried Orton.

Henriette accepted the 21-stone butcher as her son without question, so desperate was she to be reunited with the child she had loved above all others. Orton did not disappoint her. He had used his time in England well, gleaning every scrap of information he could pick up about Roger and the Tichborne family. He could not physically become Roger Tichborne but he could put up a convincing charade. Even when he made the odd mistake, such as forgetting the names of schoolteachers and school friends, Henriette chose to ignore it, saying: 'He confuses everything as in a dream.' Henriette immediately made Orton an annual allowance of £1,000. His unchallenged acceptance by Henriette made him even bolder. Now was the time, he decided, to go after the full family inheritance.

The imposter returned to England to set about claiming the family estates. He read up as much as he could about the finer details of the Tichborne history and family life. He even cheekily bounced the two-year-old twelfth baronet on his knee in a convincingly avuncular manner. And once established in Hampshire, Orton invited two old troopers of the Dragoon Guards to join the household as servants. From them, he learned all about Roger's regimental life. Finally he agreed to sign a sworn affidavit that he was indeed Roger Charles Tichborne who had had the good fortune to be rescued from the stricken *Bella* by the Australia-bound *Osprey* which had transported him to his new life. Orton even managed to convince the Tichborne family solicitor, Robert Hopkin, of the justice of his cause.

One person he did not convince, however, was Roger's loyal friend Vincent Gosport, who naturally asked Orton about the contents of the letter he had been given. Of course, Orton knew nothing of such a letter, and Gosport realised straight away that the man in front of him was an impostor. Another obvious clue to his inept deception was that he failed to recognise his former love, Kattie, and mistakenly referred to her as Katie.

Despite this drawback, Orton steadfastly pursued his claim that he was the true Sir Roger Tichborne, heir to the Tichborne estates, and the real twelfth baronet. Progress was by no means as swift as he would have liked, however, and it took four years for his claim to be heard in the Chancery Division of London's High Court. During this time, two crucial witnesses on the Tichborne side had died: Henriette and family solicitor Robert Hopkin.

Orton went to great trouble and expense to assemble his evidence, one extravagant example of which was to lead to his downfall. He travelled with a lawyer to Chile to prove that he, 'Roger Tichborne', had stayed at certain villages during his time in South America; this visit could have paid off because Orton had indeed been to South America. But he was recognised there as being plain Arthur Orton, and those who remembered him also recalled that he had been around three years before Roger Tichborne had even arrived on the scene. Orton was now digging himself an even deeper hole. For, apart from arousing the lawyer's suspicions, further details of Orton's own past came to light – including how, as a seaman, he had jumped ship in Chile and eventually turned up in Australia, where he had adopted the name Thomas Castro.

The hearing began on May 11, 1871. There were several witnesses who swore Orton was the Roger they had known either as a child or in the Dragoons: even Roger's former governess said Orton was definitely the child she had cared for. In all, Orton called 100 witnesses to support his claim. The Tichborne family could produce only seventeen. However, several pieces of evidence proved once and for all that Orton was not Roger Tichborne.

The first came from Roger's beloved Katherine Doughty, who had since married and become Lady Katherine Radcliffe. The court was hushed as she read out the letter she had kept all those years. By contrast, the court was aghast when Orton claimed that, as young sweethearts, he had feared getting Katherine pregnant – a claim that Lady Radcliffe sniffily but convincingly denied, saying they had never been lovers. Another compelling piece of evidence was the absence of a tattoo on Orton's arm because Sir Roger was known to have had one. Then there was the mystery of how 'Sir Roger' had forgotten how to play chess or to read music. There was also the question of Orton's speech, which was certainly not that of a gentleman. As Orton himself declared afterwards: 'I would have won if only I could have kept my mouth shut!'

After a hearing, which lasted 103 days, Orton was declared an impostor and was arrested and charged with perjury. With cheers ringing in his ears from those who still firmly believed he was genuine, he was released on bail. He spent the year in the run-up to his trial travelling around Britain giving talks at music halls, public meetings and church fetes. A subscription fund was set up to pay for his defence.

Orton eventually appeared in court to answer twenty-three charges of perjury. The trial lasted 188 days, the longest criminal hearing in British legal history. This time, a desperate but fiercely determined Orton called 300 witnesses, some from South America and Australia. The Crown called 210. As part of its case, the prosecution submitted a notebook which contained Orton's handwriting. He had written a strange motto: 'Some men has plenty money and no brains, and some men has plenty brains and no money. Surely men with plenty money and no brains were made for men with plenty brains and no money.'

The jury eventually decided that, whatever brains Orton thought he had, he deserved no more money or sympathy. They found him guilty and he was sentenced to fourteen years' imprisonment. He was released in 1884 after serving ten years. He sold his story to a newspaper for £3,000, finally confessing that he was plain Arthur Orton but excusing himself by saying: 'The story really built itself and in that way it grew so large that I really could not get out of it.'

It was a confession he was later to recant. But despite attempts to resurrect his career in public speaking, Orton discovered that people were no longer interested. He died in a humble boarding house, a broken man, on April 1, 1898. He was 64. To the end, the 'Tichborne Claimant', as he was now universally known, insisted on maintaining his false identity. The plaque on the lid of his pauper's coffin read: 'Sir Roger Charles Doughty Tichborne'.

The coarse butcher from Wagga Wagga might have had delusions of grandeur but he died a big fat fraud, disgraced and humiliated. The measure of his disgrace was voiced by the judge who had sentenced him, who, referring to the besmirching of Lady Katherine Radcliffe's honour, said: 'No more foul or deliberate falsehood was ever heard in a court of justice.' His final humiliation came as the result of medical evidence put before the court by his own defence counsel. They argued that Orton and Tichborne were one and the same because of the miniscule size of the conman's penis: had not Sir Roger Tichborne been nicknamed by his fellow army officers as 'Small Cock'?